D1351480

Andrew Shonfield

Europe: Journey to an Unknown Destination

An expanded version of the BBC Reith Lectures 1972

Allen Lane

337.91(4)EEC

321:04
SHO

337.91(4) EEC
SHO

327.7(4)EEC "1974"
SHO.

Allen Lane
A Division of Penguin Books Ltd,
21 John Street, London WC1

R ISBN 0 7139 0526 3

Made and printed in Great Britain by
Hazell Watson & Viney Ltd,
Aylesbury, Bucks
Printed in Linotype Baskerville

(24.9.07)

(14.2.91)

Contents

Preface

Faced with an occasion like the Reith Lectures and a subject that one has been thinking about actively for the previous fifteen years, one discovers, without surprise, that one fails to confine what one wants to say to the allotted six half-hour radio sessions. Even after what I regarded as a Herculean effort of compression, I found myself at each recording at Broadcasting House making last-minute cuts in the text, with the skilful aid of my producer, George Mac-Beth, in order to accommodate it to the time available. So I looked around for a means of presenting my ideas in a manner which did not leave me feeling quite so breathless, and this book is the result.

It is still a work of compression; I have not attempted to marshal all the evidence or to meet all the objections that could be made to the arguments that are advanced here. My aim has been to point to those events and underlying trends in the construction of Europe which I judge to be politically significant for the future. This text, then, does not depart from the spirit or tone of the 1972 Reith Lectures; it contains all that I have said in them, plus some further development of certain of the ideas, which did not lend itself readily to the summary type of exposition that is characteristic of the spoken word on radio. This is partly a limitation imposed by a form of aural impatience which most of us have and recognize; we do not want to be bothered to listen hard for the precise meaning of some qualification or elaboration of an argument that can be so easily absorbed through the written word.

It is worth saying something briefly about the spirit of my analysis of the European Economic Community and of its place in the international system. I have not applied myself at all to the argument about whether it was wise for Britain to enter the Community or not. I have been a partisan of entry for many years, and having taken an active, though minor, part in the debate which led eventually to British membership, I approached this book with the determination of enjoying the luxury of detachment. I did so in an easy spirit because I am persuaded that if the EEC seriously addresses itself to the essential purposes of the European construction which are set forth in the following pages, the British people, after some direct experience of what is involved, will not want to desert it. It is a very imperfect organization, uncertain of its aims and slow in clarifying them; indeed it is – as has been remarked about another justly maligned institution, democratic government – the worst thing of its kind, with the exception of all the others of which we have experience.

I have been helped by two people in particular in writing this book. One is François Duchene, the Director of the International Institute for Strategic Studies, who brought to bear on my first drafts of the Reith Lectures his speculative mind and imaginative perception of the deeper forces moving international relations. The other is Zuzanna Shonfield, my wife, whose keen sense both for verbal form and for the cogency of argument were applied with her usual critical vigour to the text that follows; whatever demerits remain, I know that it is a good deal better than it would have been without the work that she put into it.

A. S.
December 1972

1

Melting-Pot or
Bag of Marbles

At the climax of the great debate on British entry into the European Community the argument sometimes sounded something like this. One side was saying that the whole operation was a disgraceful and unnecessary surrender of national power to conduct our own affairs – unnecessary because the European Community was essentially a feeble thing which would, if we only let it be, go away. And the other side, while urging us to brace ourselves for a great historic decision, told us authoritatively not to worry because the Community really had remarkably little power in practice to change the way in which its member states run their national affairs. Well, which is it? Feeble or powerful? Historic or a dead bore?

There are occasions when I find myself oscillating between these two views. The feebleness of the organization was very much in evidence during the bleak years of General de Gaulle's rule in the 1960s, when the French Government seemed bent on blocking any move that remotely threatened to give the Community a bit of extra authority. But even as late as 1972, under a very different French president, I was given a depressing demonstration of how this narrow view of what the Community is about continues to exercise its influence. In January 1972, when Britain was about to sign the Treaty of Accession, I happened to be in Brussels, and found that a violent argument was in progress about the precise form which the legal document should take. In particular, was the current chairman of the Council of Ministers, M. Thorn of Luxembourg, to sign on behalf of the Council, which had agreed the terms with Britain, or not? One would have thought that there could have been no doubt that he should. But the French Government representatives insisted that this had after all not been a 'Community exercise' but a negotiation between six governments acting in their own individual capacities which had simply agreed to accept a seventh into a club that they had formed. It became evident that the French attached the very greatest importance to this metaphysical distinction between what the European nations do acting together and what they do as members of the European Community. They were still battling hard to keep the Community as such out of the business of signing the treaty when I left Brussels, forty-eight hours before Mr Heath and the prime ministers of the other candidate countries were due to arrive for the ceremony.

In the end a compromise was arranged which recognized the individual status of each government signing and also registered the fact that the chairman of the Council of Ministers had some kind of status in the act. But the story has more than mere curiosity value. It was not just metaphysics. It indicates the extent to which the detailed operation of the Community powers is today being jealously observed and controlled by the member governments. This is no European melting-pot. Indeed, most of the time it looks more like a bag of marbles.

However, it is possible to show that in practice it has rather more cohesive power than that. One has to look at individual cases, and I shall use a couple of recent decisions made by the European Court of Justice. They were not exceptional decisions; I picked them out of the newspapers when they were reported in the course of a couple of weeks in the summer of 1972. In one of them a British company, ICI, was fined $50,000, and so were half a dozen other European chemical firms, because they had operated an agreement to fix the prices of certain chemical products at an artificially high level. The Community was collecting close to half a million dollars from some of the biggest firms in Europe; ICI was included, even though it is a British firm, because its trading activities in the six countries of the Community made it liable. The Community has that sort of power over people outside. The second case concerned a tax imposed by the Italian Government on the export of works of art. The Court held that the Italian Government had no right to exact such a tax on goods that were sold to other countries in the European Community, because it meant treating art buyers there worse than Italian buyers. In consequence all the money that it collected in this way from 1962 onwards is now to be disgorged by the Italian state.

As a final example, also in that same fortnight last summer: a question was raised in Brussels about the special tax reliefs and subsidies given by the British Government to industry in development areas. Were these in fact higher than the level on which the Community members had agreed for themselves, and would the result be to give an unfair competitive advantage to certain British products that would ultimately be exported duty-free to the Common Market? Britain will probably be called upon, once it is a member of the Community, to prove that this is not so.

These examples, taken almost at random as they occurred within a few days of one another in the summer of 1972, will serve as a means of exploring the *kind* of power which the Community has and its limitations. One characteristic which is common to them is that the point of contention – the issue which leads the Community to lay down the law – derives from a prior agreement among the member states *not* to do certain things: not to rig prices, not to tax trade with another Community country, not to use subsidies for development areas to gain an unfair commercial advantage. In fact, the Community in its original form was largely built around the idea of a compact of abstention: governments agreed to get rid of all tariffs on trade among the member states and then to abstain from interference with the free movement of goods, of persons, and of money, within their combined territory. Now, agreeing on a number of specific things that governments will not do is much easier than arriving at a positive agreement on a line of action to be taken in common. That is no doubt one of the reasons why the first stages of West European integration, when the six countries concentrated on getting rid of petty government regulations which impeded movement between them, went with such a swing. This was surely their finest hour, and the old hands in Brussels speak of it still with nostalgia – as if they had only to recapture this early innocence and enthusiasm in order to be able to repeat the great victories in the changed circumstances of the 1970s. They do not know how they got separated from their Garden of Eden; they are not conscious of having succumbed to temptation; and now they just wander about unhappily looking for an antidote to the serpent's bite which got them unawares.

But the truth is that the situation itself is, and has been for some time, profoundly different from what it was. And it is not just the fault of de Gaulle – or whatever the serpent was called. After the first energetic bout of cleaning up, the Community members had to get down to the more difficult and laborious task of agreeing on the details of the new structure that they wanted to build for themselves. To take a concrete case: it was not enough to lay down the general principle that subsidies to development areas were not to be used on such a scale as to give producers in any one area an unfair competitive advantage in their export trade to other member states; there had to be agreement about the permitted scale itself and also about a set of common rules to guide the behaviour of governments. And that is bound to be a complicated business when claims for special treatment may vary all the way from those of the poor peasants of southern Italy to those of the beleaguered burghers of Berlin.

The Technocratic Approach

So the Community finds itself back in the business of making regulations, just like the national governments, and with the added complication that it has to cover the needs of several different nations in formulating each of its rules. It is plodding work; and in addition to being laborious, the results, when they come, are very unexciting. If, for example, you want to make sure that all the beer drinkers of the Community have a free and equal choice among the beers produced in the different member countries, and are not prevented from exercising this choice by local by-laws laying down special standards, then you first have to get an agreed definition of what is beer and of its different varieties. It is surprising how many of these varieties there are ... Very unexciting work – and besides, a kind of natural catchment area for music-hall jokes. It is extraordinary what intensity goes into these arguments about definitions of types of beer and suchlike – not to mention wines, which arouse even more violent, southern passions.

Then why bother with this kind of detail? Does it matter in the end? The answer to that is that these details when added together do affect a substantial segment of people's lives. And they are not the kind of details that can be left as loose ends; if the Community does not take responsibility for making a single common rule, then the individual governments will produce a number of rules of their own, some of which will conflict with each other. Finally – and this is really the important point – the European system, as a piece of political machinery, depends on the constant testing of the collective will of the member countries to tackle any and every source of friction between them. When it comes to the big decisions, agreement often depends on a package deal involving a large number of apparently small matters, some of which happen to loom quite large in a particular nation's local politics. Wine is an outstanding example in France; beer in Belgium and Germany; you might lose an election on them if you got the answer wrong.

This then is at the back of the complaint which is so often heard, that the Community is too 'technocratic'. The people who run it are technocrats, and they have got to be. It is worth reflecting further on the meaning of this for contemporary politics at large, because technocracy is a fact about the life of all advanced industrial societies, not merely about the Community. More and more, political decisions have a technical character involving specialist knowledge about the management of some aspect of society. This is not the only thing, by any means, but it is a very important element of the modern political process which so often involves detailed and expert bargaining between different interest groups. More and more, as the Community has become engaged in the management of private power whose reach extends beyond the limits of the nation-state, its technocratic character has been reinforced. The Community started out with the notion that its main task was to secure the accord of these governments on a simple *code of abstention*. Once the governments had promised not to interfere with the operations of the free market, the forces of competition were to be relied upon to do the rest. But that was a very short-lived pipe-dream, largely, I think, of American inspiration – American with a particular Jeffersonian bias. The problem as it presents itself today is how to secure the public interest through the control and sometimes through the active mobilization of enterprises and groups of people which straddle national frontiers.

The term used for the phenomenon that I am describing is 'transnational relations' – meaning relations between people in different countries which largely bypass the effective control of the central governments of each of them. It is not that these governments would necessarily find it impossible to interfere with these activities if they were determined to do so. But it would be difficult for them; and if they did successfully interfere, that in turn could produce some unpleasant side-effects which they would be unable entirely to control.

The reason why there are these special risks which make governments doubtful about their own capacity to exercise ultimate control is precisely the fact that these transnational relations are by now so widespread. If you manage to impose a restriction on one of them, then it is quite likely that something else with an effect very similar to that which you were trying to prevent will go forward by another transnational route. What I am contending is that the Western industrial nations are by now so intermeshed with one another at so many different levels that it grows increasingly difficult for a single national government on its own to exercise effective power over many of the actions of its citizens. In these circumstances it has a choice of three options. It could insist none the less on its exclusive national sovereignty and inflict highly unpopular restraints and controls on the people that it governs; or it could opt out of exercising any kind of public power over these private interests; or it could enter a Community of nations, aiming to exercise such public power jointly.

Conditions for Membership of the Community

But why a Community – and why Europe? Surely a straightforward international agreement between governments would do just as well? The answer to that is: yes, in principle there is no reason why this new type of supranational power should not be exercised jointly by, say, France and Australia and the United States. But in practice big political decisions of this kind are not made in common unless a number of other, mainly historical, circumstances are present too. Chief of these are that the political leaders of the nations concerned should be convinced that they have a wide range of everyday problems in common, with enough understanding and sympathy for each other's approaches to make it possible to tackle them together and arrive at common solutions. And secondly that they are happy with the idea that their national desires and ambitions for as far ahead as they can see should be worked out jointly with these particular partners, *who will collectively be in a majority*. Now these are portentous conditions. They mean for example that it was inconceivable that Britain would have entered into an effective partnership with Western Europe until it had first lost its Empire and then become finally disabused of the idea of the Commonwealth as the fulcrum of an independent British policy. It also means that the Americans with a quite different view both of the capacity and of the long-term role of their nation in the world are not yet ready to contemplate the conscious sacrifice of independence that goes with membership of a Community of the European type – that is a group of nations aiming at the joint exercise of public power over a widening range of everyday activities that have hitherto been regarded as the exclusive preserve of the sovereign national state.

In order to be willing to engage in this sort of exercise a nation must not be too large. It also needs to feel vulnerable. I think that the absence of this feeling of reduced size and increased vulnerability in Britain in the period immediately following the war, when the Europeans took their first step towards integration, amply explains why the British were quite uninterested in joining in at that time. Morever I suspect that if we had been persuaded to put our signatures to some pact like the Schuman Plan[1] in that period we would have been a drag on the whole process, slowing it down because we were not convinced that the operation was really necessary. The Europeans, who were convinced, were, in my view, very wise to go ahead without us. There is nothing like a series of balance-of-payments crises for making a nation feel vulnerable, and these certainly played a big part in bringing Britain round by the 1960s to the European point of view.

1. The European Coal and Steel Community proposed by Robert Schuman, French Minister of Foreign Affairs, and formed by the Treaty of Paris, 1951.

The intermeshing of national interests and the consequent loss of control by national governments show up most clearly in international trade and payments. In Western Europe many nations export between a third and a half of their total manufacturing output. It is obviously a matter of common concern to them that the resources that they put into this activity and the employment that it provides should not be suddenly disrupted by the wilful behaviour of one or more of their neighbours. A very substantial part of their export trade is with other nations in Western Europe. It therefore makes obvious good sense not only to get rid of the tariffs and the other artificial obstacles to commerce in Western Europe, but also to establish an agreed set of rules about such matters as internal taxes and subsidies, which have a way of affecting external trade, and also about the kind of protective measures that may be employed by any member state which runs into a balance-of-payments deficit that spells trouble for its trading partners.

So the abolition of tariffs and the creation of a customs union is only the beginning. The fact is that, while the modern state has grown vastly more effective in looking after the welfare needs of its individual citizens, its ability to conduct independent national policies in the face of the new pressures coming out of the international system has been much diminished. We see this for example in the way in which very large sums of money hurtle from one country to another as soon as a particular currency comes under suspicion. Governments are no longer able to carry on the struggle to preserve the international value of their money in the old style, when they may find, as Britain did during the sterling crisis in the summer of 1972, that more than a third of the national currency reserves have gone abroad in the course of normal dealings in the foreign-exchange markets in under a week. In short, the dramatic improvement in communications, the greatly increased mobility of people and money, and also the huge concentrations of corporate power in the hands of international businesses, taken together, demand the establishment of a new dimension of international public power. At the same time there is a parallel movement, less obvious but beginning to be significant, among associations of private and professional persons – farmers, trade unionists, certain scientists, even specialist professional civil servants – who find that the natural links for much of what they wish to accomplish are with their professional colleagues abroad, rather than with their own national governments. The transnational lobbies that are thus created look for some international political counterpart.

Supranationality Redefined

Now I call this amalgam of private groups and agencies transcending national frontiers, together with the official political agencies that have been established in and around the European Community, 'supranational'. But I am not using the term in the simple, old-fashioned sense of standing *above* national governments. Bits and pieces of the national governments are themselves part of the system; so are some of the parliaments and the businesses and the professional organizations. If, to return to the simile I used earlier, this is more like a bag of marbles than a melting-pot, the marbles are soft on the surface and made of some sticky substance, like putty, which keeps them clinging together as they are pushed around and constantly make contact with one another inside the bag. It does not sound very attractive; it certainly is not very coherent. It is much less satisfactory to describe than the simplified version of a supranational European government which was the ideal of the founding fathers of the Community.

And that is one of the problems which afflict the men who run the European institutions in Brussels. They still see themselves in some measure as the guardians of an imaginary Ark of the Covenant – the embodiment of the supranational ideal which inspired M. Schuman to launch the original plan to set up a European Coal and Steel Community. If one looks back at the language used at that time, one can see that they have some excuse for their attitude. For instance in inviting Britain in 1950 to join in what were only the preliminary discussions on the scheme for a European Coal and Steel Community, M. Schuman laid it down as a condition that 'it is essential that [the proposed authority] should be independent both of government and of individual interests'.[2]

2. See Richard Mayne, *The Recovery of Europe: from Devastation to Unity*, 1970.

One senses the mood. This was the moment, only five years after
the end of the war, when a French Government, taking its courage
in both hands, was proposing a permanent Franco-German alliance based on the creation of a new kind of international authority, which would protect Europe from the machinations of any
wicked power that might arise in Germany in the future.

There were strong motives for the outright surrender of bits of
national power that had been cherished in the past. France was
scared by the prospect of the revived industrial might of Germany,
and the Germans for their part, who were still under allied occu-
pation, were eager to seize the opportunity offered to work their
passage back to international respectability. Encouraged by their
first success, with the Coal and Steel Community, the European
federalists next tried to hustle the French Government into a military agreement to amalgamate its national forces in a single European army. Again, one gets the flavour of their extraordinary
ambitions when one reads in the draft of the scheme for the European army that one of its functions was to be to maintain 'constitutional order and democratic institutions in the territories of the
member countries'. One has a vision of French soldiers marching
over the Alps to counter a Neo-Fascist march on Rome!

The remarkable thing is that one finds still today among the
Europeans of the old school, who occupy many of the seats of
power in Brussels, a common belief that they almost brought off
this decisive manoeuvre – indeed that it was only the perfidy of M.
Mendès-France, who was French Prime Minister at the time, and
his lack of devotion to the European ideal which denied them
their victory. Poor Mendès is still the object of personal hostility
for these people, many of whom are otherwise sympathetic to his
political ideas. It is strange that feelings remain so intense eigh-
teen years after the event. The reason is that the rejection of the
European Defence Community by the French Parliament in 1954
symbolizes something for the federalists: it represents the decisive
failure of their favourite post-war strategy. *La fuite en avant*, they
called this strategy, which means roughly: 'headlong flight into
an unknown future, in order to escape from a fearful present.'
They of course believed that they knew what the future would
really be – a fully federal Europe.

Traditionally, federations are made by wars – or, if not, as in the case of nineteenth-century Switzerland, by fear of war-like neighbours. The Swiss Cantons, in 1867, having had a nasty taste of Louis Napoleon on the one side and not relishing the prospect of facing Bismarck's new military power in Germany on the other, decided to surrender some of their cherished independent power to a central authority. In the Europe of the 1950s it was thought by some that the combined effect of the cold war with Russia and the need to create a re-armed Germany so soon after the end of the last war might have a similar effect. It is just possible that this might have happened, if Soviet Russia had been more openly aggressive and West Germany less orderly and manageable. But the opportunity for the 'flight into the future' quickly passed.

And now we have to try to create a modern surrogate for a federation without the benefit of war or even a serious threat of war in Europe. It is a unique exercise, because it means that every step has to be conducted by agreement between states. There is no means of coercion other than moral pressure. That is what makes this European enterprise a 'journey to an unknown destination'. Unlike the old-style European federalists, we don't know what the final answer will look like – or even should look like. But in any case it is not, in my view, the point of arrival at a final union which it is important, or even possible, to foresee; it is the joint decision to embark on the enterprise and then the experiences along the route that matter.

Limited Choice of Partners

We can say, however, something about the conditions that will have to be fulfilled if the venture is to have a reasonable chance of going forward. What is perhaps the most important of these conditions is not to be found anywhere in the basic Treaty of Rome or in other official documents of the Community. But it is implicit in what I might term the philosophy of building a Community, which I set out earlier. The institutions of the Community, on this view, are not instruments designed by a unique and irreversible act of will to carry out a clearcut common purpose, but rather the expression of a set of common circumstances continuously shaping the societies of all the member nations. If one of the members were suddenly to decide to adopt a radically different set of social and political objectives, that would create enormous difficulties for the whole enterprise. The same would be true if the conditions of daily social life took on an entirely different form in one of these countries – for instance, if one of the national governments were faced with such strong opposition from its citizens that it could no longer enforce the law, except by the constant use of police violence.

It is obvious why in the latter case such a state would be a very poor partner in the building up of a Community. For one thing it could not give a reasonable assurance to its partners that the compromises and bargains with them which it made now would be fulfilled a year hence. The first rule therefore is that a Community depends on having national governments which do in fact govern, and that the process of governing must be based on a large degree of continuity of public support. A one-party state like Spain would for this reason, among others, be an impossible partner, In any case, so much in the building of the Community depends on the spontaneous activities of independent interest-groups operating freely across national frontiers that dictatorships cannot be accommodated. But on purely practical grounds it would be vastly inconvenient, to put it no higher than that, if in any dealings with the Spanish Government the others had constantly to be saying to themselves: 'And is this one of the bargains that will be kept when General Franco dies and is replaced by goodness knows whom?'

The other point – the need for the actual conditions of life and the social assumptions behind them to remain broadly in conformity among all the nine future members of the European Community – is a more complicated one. It is not suggested that there is no room for differences in social policy. The Germans, for instance, have a much more generous old-age-pension scheme, and spend far more on it, than most of their partners. The British have invested more of their resources in the National Health Service. There is no reason why this should cause conflict. But consider, for example, what would happen if one of the countries moved sharply to the right and decided that the state should drastically reduce its financial responsibility for matters connected with the social welfare of its poor citizens. Say it adopted a reform to make everyone, including the poor, pay the going commercial rate of insurance for social security; since the poor are naturally high risks they would have to pay more than others and this would result in greater social inequality. It would then be very hard for the other nations, with their established policies of public responsibility for welfare, graduated income tax, pursuit of more equality, and so on, to work out common positions with the country in question. Inevitably, a number of subjects would arise – pensions, taxes, safety and health regulations – on which it would be necessary, but almost impossible, to collaborate. The Community could hardly manage to move forward with this country as a partner.

But now look at the matter from the other end of the political spectrum – the case not of a reactionary right-wing government in pursuit of inequality, but of an extreme left-wing one, aiming at a rapid and profound re-distribution of wealth and income. Here the open frontiers of the Community, the agreements to abstain from impeding the movement of people, goods and money, would greatly complicate the political problem. The danger would be that, for example, an exceptionally heavy tax designed to discriminate sharply against company profits or the ownership of capital would induce the people who felt they were being badly treated to move their resources to other, more friendly, parts of the Community. A single national government on its own would find it very hard to stand up against this.

There are other reasons why a major deviation in social and economic policy by one country, whether to the left or to the right, would be impeded by the complex of social and political forces which make up the European Community. I do not of course mean one of the familiar shifts of political power from main-line conservatives to main-line social democrats or vice versa. The Community has never found any problem with these. The doubt would apply more to a West European version of Castro's Cuba or to the government of the colonels in Greece. This perhaps explains why socialists of the extreme left who insist on the revolutionary option have always tended to be instinctively hostile to the Community idea. The bizarre alliance of Michael Foot, a radical of the left, and Enoch Powell, a radical of the right, during the debates on British entry becomes more explicable on these grounds.

But how important is it in practice to the socialist left to keep the revolutionary option open? Reference to my central argument about the reasons for the emergence of the European Community will explain my doubts. These derive from the view of the Community as the expression of a common fact of international life – the fact that the advanced industrial countries of Western Europe are today in an increasingly exposed and vulnerable position and that they are less and less in charge of their individual national destinies. We live with more international constraints on our freedom of political action than many politicians care to recognize publicly. Giving up the revolutionary option by joining an international group which deliberately accepts these constraints will, in my view, be lamented chiefly for the loss of a favourite form of rhetoric, rather than for any practical effect that it may have on the actions of the socialist parties of Western Europe.

2

The French Spirit
and the British Intruder

Thinking about the way in which national attitudes make their
mark on European Community politics, I recall an occasion when
I was taken to task in Brussels for the excessive Englishness of my
approach to European institutions. I was at the time a member of
a committee set up by the European Commission, the Vedel Committee, to work out a set of proposals for strengthening the European Parliament. After some months of argument we had reached
agreement, in early 1972, on the main outlines of a scheme, and
then went on to discuss possible ways of giving the European
Parliament some immediate practical power without waiting for
the laborious business of amending the Treaty of Rome. It seemed
to me fairly simple for the Council of Ministers, which at present
wields all the effective power, to engage in a formal act of self-
denial – to say that henceforth it would not make certain kinds of
European laws without the prior agreement of the Parliament in
Strasbourg. I presented an argument on these lines to our committee in Brussels, and very likely I made it all seem too facile. But
that was not the point. What grated on the French chairman,
M. Vedel – an extremely articulate and witty man, and incident-
ally something of an admirer of Britain and British ways – was a
certain loose pragmatism in my whole approach. Wagging his
finger at me in a monitory fashion he said something like this (I
am paraphrasing): 'What you British will have to learn when you
are in the Community is what it means to live inside a precisely
defined legal system. The Community is in its very essence a system
of laws. Once a particular responsibility has been transferred by
law to an identified agency of the Community, that agency does
not have the right to hand it over to anyone else. It cannot share
a responsibility that was given to it alone.'

Now what lay behind my chairman's sharp intervention was his sense that the British were particularly disinclined to understand the important distinction between a nation, which exists apart from its constitutional laws, and an entity like the European Community whose very being is its legal system. I think he was quite right to be a little worried about this. So much of British public life is a matter of unwritten understandings and of a willingness to adjust these to changing circumstances. Indeed there is a fear of being too precise in distributing powers and responsibilities among different public bodies, instead of leaving them to work things out together. Our experience of the working of the political system is that behaviour changes in response to altered circumstances, and then laws are formulated to give extra precision and reliability to practices that are already in process of being established.

The experience of most of the members of the European Community is very different. One has to remember that two of them, Germany and Italy, are nations that acquired their political identity only in the late nineteenth century. They are used to thinking of constitutional laws as the essential means of expressing the identity of the nation. One might almost say that without these laws there would be some doubt whether the nation as a political entity existed at all. In France the case is of course different: the nation, like the British nation, is old. But the question of the legitimacy of national government, how far it has the right, as well as the power, to demand the obedience of its citizens, has exercised an extraordinary influence over French history and thinking for the past two centuries. One government after another has felt compelled to spell out explicitly the rights of citizens in terms which then make it impossible for the government legally to perform a number of actions. If the courts are faced with an official action which is covered by regular legislative authority but which infringes any of these rights, they will find the government at fault and refuse to carry out the instructions of the legislature. It is not parliament that is sovereign but the body of constitutional laws which defines the authority of parliament, along with that of various other agencies set up to safeguard the public interest and execute the national will. It is clear that the interpreters of the law, the judges in the courts, have a different *political* weight and significance in a constitutional set-up of this kind. And this is essentially the same set-up as that of the European Community.

European versus British Law

The kind of problem that this could pose can be seen in its starkest form if one imagines a situation in which a law recently enacted by the British Parliament was shown, in the course of some litigation in the courts, to contradict some earlier piece of Community law. A British judge might then have to decide that Parliament had gone beyond its powers in passing the later Act and that it was not to be obeyed. Of course the British courts would be expected to interpret Acts of Parliament in such a way as to make them as far as possible consistent with Parliament's decision to abide by European Community law. But in the last resort it would be the courts, the interpreters of the law, who would decide whether an Act of Parliament was to be obeyed or not.

Now this kind of conflict is a most especially difficult one for the British, because of the peculiar character of European Community law. So much of the latter is concerned with supplying the building bricks for a European structure that has not yet come fully into existence; it is the extreme opposite to the spirit of English laws, which traditionally are, as I have said, concerned with enacting as rules of behaviour practices that are already widely accepted. In Britain legal fact generally follows on social practice. The Community's laws on the other hand make sense for the most part because they are seen as pieces of a larger design of common European policies, which is aimed at by member countries, but which will only become a fact at some future date. It follows that in the interpretation of Community law the *intentions* of the legislators are all-important. But British judges are simply not concerned with any evidence about what those who made the law in Parliament really intended. They look at the literal meaning of the words; that is all. In the European Court of Justice aims count more than words.

If one reflects about it, one can readily see why any political construction which emerges out of a deliberate act of will – the founding of a new nation, the setting up of a federation of a

number of states, the making of a revolutionary constitution –
must be of this kind. They are all looking ahead to something
which will be deeply different from the present in a variety of
ways that have yet to be explored in practice. They depend heavily
on statements of general principle and on agreements about broad
objectives. As we have seen in the United States (which is just such
a political construction) the Supreme Court which ultimately has
the task of interpreting these principles fulfils in some periods of
history an extremely radical function – pushing the interpretation
of Federal laws well beyond the consensus view of the American
public. This has been notably so in asserting the civil rights of
American blacks during the post-war period. The law in this case
becomes an instrument in the struggle to fulfil the intentions that
were implicit in the original act of will which set up the political
structure. These intentions may not have been explicitly formulated by the founding fathers or consciously understood by a
majority of the people at the time. Thus, to use one of Rousseau's
favourite distinctions, the law is an expression of the *volonté
générale* rather than of the *volonté de tous*.[1] One finds the same
kind of function being performed by the courts in non-federal
states like France, where certain fundamental laws about the conduct of the state towards its citizens derive from the revolutionary
statement of principles contained in the Declaration of the Rights
of Man. Some important decisions giving the ordinary person increased protection against the growing might of governmental
power have come out of that process in recent years.

How is one to explain the tenacity of the quite different British
tradition? Its defenders would no doubt point out, quite fairly,
that it has not been notably less efficient in safeguarding the liber-
ties of the individual. I think the deeper answer lies in a basic
assumption which affects so many aspects of British public life;
it is that we live in a very homogeneous society. This conviction
is, I suspect, so deeply embedded in our minds that we are rarely
prompted even to think about it. But if one considers some of the
most characteristic and precious elements of British practice – for
example the fact that in the face of considerable risks the police,
exceptionally in this country, continue to go about their ordinary

1. See *Le Contrat social*.

duties unarmed – it becomes evident at once that they would make no sense at all unless it were assumed that the overwhelming mass of people were in active agreement in wanting to maintain the same basic set of rules.

That is plainly not an assumption that can be made in a very heterogeneous society like the United States. Indeed the whole American approach to law is coloured by the aim of achieving a modus vivendi with the minimum of trouble among people who are expected to be very heterogeneous. Of course the British principle is much more comfortable to live with. But there is a price to be paid. It takes time for general standards of behaviour to evolve spontaneously in desired directions; and waiting may be expensive when the conditions of society are themselves changing very rapidly. It should be noticed, further, that when a heterogeneous element was introduced into our society, as a result of large-scale Commonwealth immigration, it was found necessary to change the *style* of law-making in order to cope with the problem. The Race Relations Act is more like the tutelary kind of law, of the non-British type; it looks to the establishment of more exacting standards of behaviour than those which were current when the law was passed and it penalizes people for doing and saying things which would encourage others not to accept these standards. More recently, the Industrial Relations Act of 1972 seems to fall into a similar category; at any rate, it depends on the acceptance of new *norms* of behaviour on the part of organized labour, quite different from those which are generally accepted today. So perhaps the demands which will be made on Britain by the European Community style of law-making will not, after all, come as a complete shock.

The Barrier of French Legalism

There is another side of the legalistic approach to the European Community, pressed particularly by the French, which seems to me much more doubtful. The French Government's view is that in signing the Treaty of Rome it accepted a number of limited commitments about the way in which certain named aspects of economic policy were to be run. Beyond that there is a general desire to establish a political construction for Western Europe, but, the French insist, to realize that desire will require a separate and deliberate act of will on the part of the member states. Without that act of will, they feel no obligation to increase the scope of the Community's activities or to endow its institutions with any more responsibility. On the contrary they are the keenest and most watchful opponents of any extension of the authority of the European Commission. But more of that later.

The general point is that whereas the French constitutional and legal experience helped to make them a powerful force in the first phase of the construction of Europe, it has subsequently made them notably rigid in their interpretation of the manner in which this novel and quite unfamiliar organization of states is to be allowed to develop further. As so often, one finds that differences of view about the way to organize international relations are dominated by the accidents of domestic national history. What the French seem to have in mind is that before Europe can go on to the next stage of making a political construction to match the European Economic Community, it will need to decide to bring into being a constitution-making body – a constituent assembly of the type used in the French Revolution and after – which will then provide the member states with the occasion for a single over-riding political decision. This will mean that certain powers hitherto wielded by the states separately will be surrendered by them irrevocably to a superior authority expressing the collective will of the Community.

It will be seen that this whole approach imputes to the institutions which the Community needs and is trying to construct a simple kind of supranationality – based on authority and unquestioned dominance – which, as indicated in Chapter 1, I regard as entirely unrealistic. If that is so, the imputation is to be seen as a way of avoiding the practical issue.

The British Government fortunately comes into the Community without any of the ideological baggage which still clutters up the people who took part in the heroic first phase of the great enterprise. The British, above all, do not believe easily in short cuts. The Governments, both Labour and Conservative, which decided in the 1960s that it was worth while trying to join had no illusions about achieving quick political results. But on the other hand, it was precisely the further political process that was promised by the development of the European Community which attracted Britain. It is interesting on this point to look back at Mr Heath's Godkin Lectures, which he gave in the United States while he was in opposition.[2] His theme was the new Europe, and his focus was chiefly on matters which went well beyond the Treaty of Rome and the straightforward economics of the Common Market – on European defence and strategy and on Western Europe's prospects as a world monetary power. He seemed to be looking for precisely those open-ended commitments which the French so dislike. I think that he reflects a genuine feeling in this country: the British will be frustrated if the European Community fails to be an effective political force in world affairs, in just the sense that it has not been one to date. In that respect Britain is different from most of the existing members. Its views on the ultimate purpose and political scope of a limited international group like the European Community seem likely in the long run to be more akin to Germany's than to the others. There is much more concern in both countries about the impact of this new Europe on the world outside – whether it is focused on the Soviet world in the German case or on the Atlantic world in the British one – than about the details of precisely how and to what extent the member states will compound their inevitable domestic differences amongst themselves.

The Function of Majority Voting

If the Community as a whole tends to adopt a similar perspective – as I think it will increasingly during the 1970s – then it will have to develop a capacity to make joint decisions beyond that which it now possesses. How is it to achieve this? One answer to the question given by the European federalists is that all would have been well if only the Community had stuck to the principle of majority voting, and had not been forced to surrender to the French, who opposed it – and further, that all will be well again

2. Harvard Godkin Lectures on *The Essentials of Free Government and the Duties of the Citizen*, 1967.

once the French are induced to lift their veto. This refers back to the bitter struggle which took place in the latter part of 1965, when General de Gaulle carried his opposition to certain ideas put forward in Brussels to the point of withdrawing French official representatives from all meetings of Community bodies. The deadlock lasted for half a year. Although the French policy of 'the empty chair' did not in the end bust the Community, it shook it badly.

By early 1966 everyone was desperately eager for a compromise, which the French duly conceded – on certain conditions. They too had been shaken by the unexpected solidarity of the other five partners, under discreet German leadership, in the face of threats and sulks in Paris. One of their conditions was that in future no decisions would be taken on a majority vote on any matter which they, the French, or indeed any of the other nations, regarded as an important national interest. The form of words agreed in the celebrated Luxembourg compromise of January 1966 simply registered the fact that the French held to their view on majority voting, while the others took the line that in any case the Community countries would never in practice try to out-vote one of their number on any subject which it regarded as a vital national interest.

There is no doubt that the other five countries, who were really saying that there was no need for the French to fuss and fret about this anyway, were giving a realistic account of the facts of Community life. Since there is no means of coercion against any government which defies a majority ruling, it follows that it would be remarkably foolish to put a nation in a minority of one and force a decision on it against the manifest will of the majority of its voters. It would simply be inviting them to turn their government out of office and get the decision blocked or reversed. In a confrontation between a majority of voters in one country and a majority of governments in the Community, the voters ultimately have the upper hand. That is why everyone knows that the confrontation is not worth risking.

What has turned out to be damaging about the Luxembourg compromise of 1966 is that it has formalized and reinforced some bad political habits in the Community. Whereas it was recognized beforehand that there were severe practical limits to majority voting in the Council of Ministers, it was used as a convenient means of exerting moral pressure on particular states in certain situations. Sometimes the governments of the states concerned were quite willing in the last resort to go back to their own people with a decision that they did not particularly like and say to them: 'We are sorry about this; but we tried and were out-voted.' But nowadays everyone knows that you are never out-voted unless you actively want to be. The result is that, in all but the most insignificant matters, the Community operates in practice under the most severe form of veto system, reminiscent of the *liberum veto* of the Polish Parliament in the seventeenth and eighteenth centuries. And it is worth recalling just how ineffective that was in handling Poland's external relations, most especially in coping with neighbours who wanted it divided.

To deal with this weakness what is now required is not some formal grand reversal of the positions adopted in Luxembourg in 1966, but rather a more workaday process of reviving the spirit of systematic compromise on which the major achievements of the early days of the Community were built. What is most insidious and destructive in an association of this kind is a practice by the members of treating each case that comes before them strictly on its individual merits. In that way they are driven to concentrate their attention on the effect that each such decision might have on any conceivable national interest. The Community process of legislation is then treated less and less as a series of building bricks, each making its contribution towards the ultimate political structure; instead each brick is examined in isolation – and seen to have potentially sharp edges.

It is in this particular context that so much depends on the performance of Britain as a new member of the Community. Hitherto the important business of the group has been managed to a large extent as if it were a diarchy of France and Germany – or, more precisely, a condition for any significant Community decision was that France wanted it and could obtain the agreement of Germany to it. Most of the time, on most matters, the Germans have been willing to oblige. The long-term danger to the Community, in my view, was the gradual alienation of Germany from the exercise.

Whatever the French Government may have intended, the general effect of its tactics in recent years has been to appear to be constantly putting a pistol to its partners' heads. The French threat worked because, in truth, the whole Community enterprise had depended on French initiatives and it was impossible to conceive of a Community functioning without France. The entry of Britain changes that. Potentially it liberates the other members from a particular form of blackmail. Not that Britain will constantly be ganging up with others against France; that is not how it is likely to work. It is simply the fact that a system run by three major nations is deeply different from a diarchy; no one of the three will be able to make the ultimate assumption about its own indispensability. The whole tone of the dialogue will be different – and here it is the French tone which is important. All this assumes, however, that the British come in with the aim of building up the Community as a significant force in the world at large, and not merely in the hope of using it as a device for pursuing short-term national advantages. Two big nations doing that in the European Community would certainly wreck it.

Equally, it is a mistake to suppose that this is a moment for large political gestures purporting to surrender national sovereignty. What is required now, it seems to me, is a sustained effort to use and adapt the existing institutions of the European Community for somewhat different purposes from those which the founding fathers had in mind when they wrote the Treaty of Rome. Having recognized that there is no short cut to a European federation, indeed that we may never arrive at a federal Europe, we should concentrate on what we have got, above all on developing the practice of systematic compromise in Community Europe, and make the latter as effective as possible.

The Role of the European Commission

Unfortunately, in pursuing this line of approach, one very soon comes up against a large ideological roadblock. It is one which expresses the conflict between the first generation of European federalists and the practitioners of latter-day European politics. It is not that the federalists refuse to practise the politics of compromise and bargaining between national interests – some of them are very good at it – but they regard it as very much a temporary second-best. Specifically, they point out that at the heart of the Community as conceived by the founding fathers of the system is the European Commission, the independent body set up in Brussels to watch over the performance of member governments in carrying out the Treaty of Rome and to press forward with new initiatives leading towards a united Europe. At the heart of the Community in real life is the Council of Ministers, composed of ministerial representatives of the member states, often major politicians in their own right, whose over-riding concern is naturally with the day-to-day business of their own governments. In Brussels it is noticeable that if one proposes almost any initiative of a European character which does not involve the European Commission in a central role, there is a tendency to dismiss it as being merely a piece of 'intergovernmental' business and not truly 'Communitarian'. It is impossible to convey in English the full flavour of the word 'Communitarian' when used in this way; it has an almost sacred quality, as if without the active leadership of the European Commission there can be no guarantee of the purity of a Community enterprise. Indeed some extremists take the view that any merely 'intergovernmental' arrangement, however good the European cause, weakens the Community because it diminishes the Commission's role.

The other side of the coin is that the European Commission has itself become the special target of French hostility. The French Government's view is that the Commission is (apart from a few specific economic functions of its own) simply the administrative organ of the Community, carrying out the decisions of the representatives of national governments when the latter come together in the Council of Ministers. No opportunity is lost in Paris to put the Commission in its place. Sometimes the conflict is bitter. The most recent case, a typical one, occurred over the preparation of the agenda for the summit meeting of European heads of government in 1972, when the French demanded that the Commission should be excluded altogether from these preliminary discussions when they were connected in any way with the political aspects of the summit. The President of the European Commission, Mr

Sicco Mansholt, was so incensed that he threatened publicly, in June 1972, that all the nine Commissioners would resign in a body. The French then relented, but only slightly.

Now it so happens that the British are instinctively suspicious of the European Commission, too – though on somewhat different grounds from the French. The French do not like it because of the way in which it seeks to compete with the independent national state. It is French nationalism which is offended. In the British case the feeling is rather that the Parliament in Westminster and the public at large can keep tabs on ministers when they make decisions in Brussels, but that the European Commission is a faceless bureaucracy which is not effectively responsible to anyone. There is no doubt that the whole conception of the Commission – a body of appointed officials who are supposed to have the independence associated with judges, combined with the skills of expert politicians in pushing governments further than they would go of their own accord towards European unity – is a difficult one to accommodate to British ideas of government and politics. (It is paradoxically very much in tune with French thinking.) The language of the Treaty of Rome makes large claims for the members of the Commission – they will, it proclaims, 'exercise their functions in complete independence in the general interest of the Community'.

One then asks how these independent spirits are recruited. The answer is that in practice the individual national governments have unrestricted rights of patronage: they each appoint one or two Commissioners for a period of four years – no one in the Community ever questions their choice – and if they are not satisfied with their performance they do not re-appoint them at the end of the period. The tendency has been in recent years for small countries to appoint big men and the big countries to appoint lesser men. One trouble, as pointed out by Professor Ralf Dahrendorf, the brilliant sociologist, who is one of the two German Commissioners, is that the European Commission is altogether too remote from the experiences and feelings of ordinary people in the Community. He elaborated the view, in two celebrated articles originally published under a pseudonym,[3] that the Commission

3. Wieland Europa, in *Die Zeit*, 9 and 16 July 1971.

was wrong to go on trying to claim exclusive rights to represent the European Community in every one of the great variety of joint activities in which the nations of Western Europe were now engaged. Other European bodies of a quite different character ought, he argued, to be encouraged to develop and play a larger independent part than they had been given hitherto in Community politics. There was an outcry in Brussels when the identity of this cogent critic of the Commission's claims to a monopoly of political leadership was revealed, and demands – which were fortunately resisted – that he should be dismissed from his post.

Dahrendorf's critique, however much it offended against the current conventional wisdom of Brussels, is most unlikely to continue to be ignored when it comes to reforming the institutions of the Community. No one questions that there will have to be reforms if the Community is to function effectively. The present arrangement which has made all the power flow to the Council of Ministers is no more satisfactory than the original idea of the European federalists, that the Commission should treat itself as the potential government of a European nation not yet fully grown. There is every reason to think that some body like the Commission will always be necessary – to point the way to new European initiatives, to mediate between governments, to do the complicated work, part technical, part diplomatic, of preparing the ground for joint European decisions. In order to do all these things the members of the Commission must have more status, not less. The Commissioners will have to be persons of considerable political weight, particularly those Commissioners who come from the big European countries. They should be people who can talk to cabinet ministers in the governments of the member states as equals, and have it in their power to cause a political fuss when necessary.

But what will not be easily tolerated in the future is the notion that the European Commission in some sense stands above politics, that it can adopt a holier-than-thou attitude towards the other elements in the construction of Europe. Once it is clear that it is only one of several instruments for that construction, with no exclusive rights over any part of it, governments will be more willing to recognize that its political capacity needs to be strengthened. Many people in the Community are hoping that Britain will help to do just that; the choice of the first two British Commissioners[4] has encouraged them to think that it will. But at the same time I would expect that the federal pretensions of the first phase of the construction of Europe – when the Commission was seen as the organizer of a benign conspiracy which would somehow create a federated Europe behind the backs of governments – will be finally scotched.

4. Sir Christopher Soames and Mr George Thomson, both former Cabinet ministers and politicians, who would be respectively natural candidates for high ministerial office in future Tory and Labour governments.

3
The American Connection –
a Grumbling Alliance

In the early days of the European Common Market, the Six managed to achieve a kind of illusion of privacy within the international system; they treated the often quite profound effects which the arrangements that they made with one another had on the rest of the world as if they were subsidiary matters, of no particular concern to them. They behaved for much of the time rather as though they were living inside a charmed circle bounded entirely by their own problems and preoccupations. The special circumstances of the later post-war period, when Europe finally withdrew from empire and experienced the longest uninterrupted run of prosperity ever, based on cultivating its own garden, certainly helped. The forward march of American world power which accompanied the European withdrawal was another factor. The Europeans acquired a sure military defence through the American nuclear umbrella; and American power, abetted to a diminishing extent by the British, supplied sufficient security for the movement of world trade to guarantee Europe's requirements of vital raw materials like oil. At the same time the American dollar provided an extremely effective international medium of exchange and a common reserve currency for the Europeans. Why should the countries forming the European Community have cared very much about what happened in the world beyond Western Europe?

Looking back, it is remarkable how long the Community was indulged in this fantasy. Of course there were protests by outsiders about some of the ways in which the internal arrangements of the Common Market affected them. But Community policies were barely influenced by these. In part no doubt this indulgence was due to the special sentiment nursed by the United States towards an enterprise which it had for long actively tried to foster.

The idea of a United States of Europe, formed in their own image, had a powerful attraction for the Americans. They were not going to be too meticulous in counting up the short-term profit and loss from the venture. Moreover they were inclined to be sympathetic, remembering their own history, to the requirements of wheeling and dealing among the member states in the process, even if some of this was at the expense of outsiders.

Meanwhile the politics of the European charmed circle led to the building up of a network of special agreements between the Community and a number of favoured states on its southern periphery. Many of these were Mediterranean countries; others were in Black Africa, former colonies of France and Belgium. What has been established as a result of all this is a fairly well defined zone of client states – more or less dependent commercial partners of the Community. To American eyes this systematic build-up of privileged trading arrangements by the Europeans, with its corollary of discrimination against the outsider, must look altogether too much like a variation on their own early federal history – a kind of commercial Monroe Doctrine for Eurafrica. Indeed European insouciance on this matter is very reminiscent of nineteenth-century America's attitude towards external relations in what it regarded as its own zone of influence.

But the historical parallel, now that it was translated into hard acts of commercial discrimination against US interests, failed to evoke the earlier American sympathy for the EEC enterprise. On the contrary, as the design of the European construction which they had helped to foster has emerged more clearly, the Americans have grown increasingly indignant about it. They feel cheated on two counts. First of all there is much less of the unified political power in the Community than they had hoped to see established. The aim of the American supporters of a united Europe was always to bring into being an effective political partner on the other side of the Atlantic who would be able to share with the United States the responsibility for major international decisions. Secondly the United States was looking for an ally in sustaining a universal system of international trade and payments with a uniform set of rules accepted by all and according equal treatment to all comers. The Americans can argue fairly that they made a number of sacrifices during the early post-war period in setting up a system of this kind, based essentially on the agreements reached at Bretton Woods in 1944. This was America's grand design for the post-war world. They now find that they face an invigorated Western Europe, owing its success partly to that grand design, which seems to be bent on a policy of discrimination against outsiders.

There is a certain irony in the historic reversal of roles between the two sides of the Atlantic. In the past, from the late nineteenth century right up to the Great Depression of the 1930s, the cult of the universal trading and financial system with free access on equal terms to all markets guided the international policies of Britain and a group of smaller European countries heavily dependent on foreign commerce. The United States for most of this time was living very much in an enclosed world of its own. It only began to break out of this in the 1930s. The habit of treating foreign trade and finance exclusively in terms of their effect on domestic politics took the Americans a long time to live down. But now, as the chief guardians of the universal order which they have helped to establish since the last war, they are faced with a Europe which is in its turn trying to use international trade to consolidate its own regional arrangements.

Even though the Europeans no longer show the extreme symptoms of the illusion of privacy, they often act as if the most important thing in the international system was their experiment in working out arrangements for trade and payments amongst themselves. These are very complicated arrangements and it is almost inevitable that when bargains are struck between member states, the interest that it is easiest to sacrifice is that of the outsider. This is the sense in which it is true that a new organization like the Community which is in process of forming itself will be 'inward-looking', and I do not believe that the entry of Britain will alter that essential fact of international life. I am not arguing that the enlarged Community will be irresponsibly unconcerned about the maintenance of the international economic system. But I think it unlikely that it will live up to American expectations.

United States Policy of Impatience

The Americans nowadays tend to take the view that it is the European Community which has been chiefly responsible for the breakdown of the world-wide economic arrangements which we call the Bretton Woods system. Now, they say, it is up to the Europeans to take the responsibility for putting something equally good in its place. If it is unlikely that Europe can or will, the main reason is that the Community is not yet the kind of body which is capable of taking decisive and sustained initiatives in the field of foreign policy. And that is the substance of the other American complaint about the slow development of the political power of the Community. As seen from the other side of the Atlantic, the Community is a valuable potential agent for high-level political decisions which has somehow got stuck at a low level of economic haggling among its members.

Recently there has been an observable sharpening of the American tone towards Europe. The United States is impatient and seems to be determined to advertise its impatience. The conduct of the four-months-long dollar crisis which was staged in the second half of 1971, with the American Secretary of the Treasury, Mr Connally, making a noisy European tour with the proclaimed intention of bullying Western Europe into a joint decision, was one clear sign of the change of mood. Through Mr Connally the United States Government took the line that it was opting out of any responsibility for the international value of the dollar; it was up to the other nations to decide how much value in terms of their own currencies they were willing to put on the dollar. And if they made the dollar too dear they would find themselves in heavy surplus with the United States and accumulating lots of dollars which they did not want. The United States did not care about that either. It was time for others to make decisions ...

No doubt there was an element of the histrionic in all this and the fact that Mr Connally's aggressive Texan style added force to the performance was no doubt foreseen. But there also seems to have been a considerable switch of policy which was spelt out in a more sober style in the special report for the President in 1971 on

United States international economic policy by Mr Peterson, now the Secretary of Commerce.[1] The point made there is that not only the content of American policies but also 'the methods of diplomacy will have to be changed'. Mr Peterson concludes: 'Our international negotiating stance will have to meet its trading partners with a clearer, more assertive version of new national interest. This will make us more predictable in the eyes of our trading partners.'

There are two questions that I want to explore. First how far is the United States likely to push its new aggressive and demanding policy towards Europe? And secondly how deeply are the Europeans likely to become divided from the United States during the 1970s in the face of this American pressure?

To make the first question concrete – is it probable that if the Americans continue to feel very frustrated by European behaviour, they will withdraw their military forces altogether from Western Europe? From a European point of view the main purpose served by the American presence is to provide a visible guarantee of the military involvement of the United States in the defence of this territory. It is important that American troops should not only be about in Europe, but should also be in some clear sense in the front line – so that any attempt by the other side to invade a piece of territory, for example to conduct a raid across the frontier in Berlin, would immediately risk engaging American military forces in battle. Thus to remove American soldiers altogether from Europe would be likely to be interpreted as meaning a weakening of the American nuclear guarantee against the Soviet Union and its allies. It would be an extreme step to take.

It is also hard to envisage the circumstances in which the United States would not wish to have some of its forces stationed on the territories of its closest military allies, who happen also to be extremely rich and economically powerful. Unless the United States ceases to be a world power, it will need to maintain substantial armed forces somewhere, and West Europe is a convenient place in which to keep some of them. Already much the greater

1. *The United States in the Changing World Economy*, by Peter G. Peterson, 1971.

part of the foreign-exchange cost incurred by the American forces in Europe is being covered by the Europeans, and no doubt the proportion will increase in future. In terms of the cost to the American budget, it is probably an economy, especially as it seems to be easier to recruit soldiers for a spell in Europe than to keep them in dull garrison towns in the United States.

The truth is that the European military establishment of the United States is a not very expensive way of maintaining the posture of a great power. Of course the establishment need not be as big as it is now. But then a cut in this force seems likely whether the Europeans cooperate with the Americans in economic policies or not.

There seem therefore to be strong reasons for thinking that the American response even to extreme friction with Western Europe would fall well short of a complete military withdrawal. A more likely outcome would be some less precise but nevertheless marked change in American behaviour towards the European Community on matters on which the Europeans are themselves divided. Hitherto the American interest in furthering European integration has meant that when the member states have had deep differences, the United States has not exploited them. On the contrary its desire to have them speak with a common voice has been the dominant motive. But there were signs during the 1971 dollar crisis that the Americans were at least contemplating the possibility of bargaining with the member countries individually, giving the favoured ones special concessions on trade. It is perhaps this kind of tactical manoeuvre which we should expect to see pursued more vigorously if friction grows in the future. It could, in certain circumstances, prove to be very damaging.

Europe as an Awkward Partner

That leads to the other question – how far the differences in the approach to major issues of economic and financial policy, which at present divide the United States and Europe, are of a fundamental character. If in spite of the close American military connection with Europe and the reasonable prospects of continuing European integration, I foresee a more difficult relationship between the two sides of the Atlantic during the period ahead, it is because of certain essential features of contemporary international economic relations. These do suggest that there are profound forces at work which are likely to make the EEC an awkward partner for the United States in economic and financial affairs, which is precisely where the strength of the Community is greatest. The United States still produces somewhat more than the combined output of the enlarged Community of nine countries, but the Nine are much more important as world traders – they are together responsible for some 40 per cent of all international trade – and they own over half of all the world's currency reserves.

There is a historic tendency on the part of the United States to see the relatively low proportion of its national income that is derived from international trade as an overwhelming source of bargaining strength. In a crisis where the United States is in disagreement with Europe on some aspect of economic policy there is a standard reflex action on the part of a substantial section of American public opinion. It crows: 'In the last resort we can opt out; you can't.' It is the visceral American reaction, recalling with satisfaction that it is after all only dealing with the bad Old World which it escaped from long ago. The reaction was much in evidence once again during the dollar crisis of 1971. In effect the line taken by the United States Treasury was that the essential strength of the dollar depended on the overwhelming productive power of the nation, which is responsible for about one third of the total measured output of the world; and if the Europeans didn't like the way the Americans were handling the dollar, they could either lump it or take their business elsewhere. The choice was a matter of indifference to the United States.

Now I believe this line of thought to be based on an American delusion. The Americans in fact lost their secluded playground some time ago. They may still be playing the same sports, and the landscape immediately in front of them may look the same; but it is now enclosed in the middle of a busy and populous city. The people outside are within shouting distance all the time. I shall not attempt to list the factors that have so greatly increased America's interdependence with the rest of the world. The most important is in any case political and psychological. The United

States is a world power, exercising authority and influence on a scale that is probably larger than has ever been done before. It cannot both be and do that, and opt out.

The way in which this is likely to impinge on European-American relations is usefully indicated by some of the conclusions reached in a recent article by a former senior economic official of the United States Government, Mr Harald Malmgren. He argues that 'Commercial and financial issues are starting to replace traditional diplomatic and security questions as the main stuff of foreign policy ...' This, he says, is partly because major wars involving a conflict between the super-powers have become improbable. The old foreign-policy questions dominated by the issue of national security become less significant. But equally important, he suggests, is that 'a sweep of world-wide economic adjustment is also under way, changing the framework of international politics.'[2] It is because the European Community, most especially in its characteristic long-term policy objectives, is such a significant part of this changing framework of international politics that I expect the problems of adjustment to be faced by the United States to be especially acute here.

Changing Conditions of International Economic Relations

This really goes back to the basic argument in Chapter 1 – that the Community is a European response to a general phenomenon which is common to all the advanced industrial countries of the Western world today. They are so exposed to events and movements taking place beyond their frontiers that the old style of foreign-policy making by separate national states no longer meets the case. It is as if several layers of skin had been removed and the nerves exposed. Naturally it is the smallest nations that become aware of this new reality first. Typically it was Holland and Belgium which pressed hardest for the creation of the European Community and which have been the most vigorous supporters of integration. The medium-sized nations of around the fifty-million population mark, like France, Germany and Britain, took a little

2. 'Managing Foreign Economic Policy', in the journal *Foreign Policy*, No. 6, Spring 1972.

longer to learn the truth. A nation fashioned on a continental scale, like the United States, will take a longer time yet.

The delay is entirely understandable, since the new conditions of international economic life are only in process of emerging. It was not that the members of the European Community were more far-sighted than the Americans; they were, after their experience in the last war, that much more nervous. They invented something for one set of purposes, of which the reconciliation of Germany with France was thought to be the most important, and found themselves with an instrument which was potentially capable of dealing with a much wider range of problems of contemporary international life.[3]

The point is most readily made by some concrete examples. Nowadays governments, local as well as national governments, spend on an entirely different scale from anything known in the past. There is a huge market here running from military hardware to the construction of new towns, and in the developed countries the great bulk of it bypasses the ordinary channels of international trade. Moreover this kind of business is likely to grow, as public welfare policies emerge as the decisive element in large-scale investment projects, most especially in the advanced integrated transport systems, in the production of energy and in communications.

Next, consider the increasing number of goods and services that are sold by commercial firms which have to conform to exacting standards set by governments as part of the effort to safeguard individual and social welfare. Anti-pollution standards are an immediate case in point, which will surely grow in importance. Safety standards are another. Thus the fact that the United States is bringing in a new set of regulations on motor safety which will have to be met by every new car that is sold there is already producing repercussions in the European motor industry. The general point here, of which safety standards are only an illustration, is that the sale of goods across national frontiers is nowadays impeded less by straightforward tariffs, which in any case are now

3. It is worth recording, however, that Jean Monnet, the most far-sighted of the founding fathers of the European Community, was clear from the beginning that they were forging a new instrument of international relations at large.

relatively low, than by a variety of official and unofficial obstacles of a more subtle kind, which are labelled collectively 'non-tariff barriers'.

It is not only a matter of technical standards whose effect, whether intentional or not, is often to help the local producer to capture the market. (This includes health regulations which affect trade in foodstuffs.) There are more subtle ways in which the direction of international trade is determined by factors other than straightforward competitive power in a free market. The international market is in fact very far from free. It is remarkable how large a part of international trade in manufactured goods consists of transactions between subsidiaries or affiliates of one and the same company which are located in different countries. Investigations done in Britain and America (which are admittedly the two countries with the highest level of overseas investment) indicate that as much as a quarter of all industrial exports consists of goods moving on such interior lines of communication within companies crossing national frontiers. Such foreign commerce, which is the result of a transfer between two partners in a single enterprise rather than of a conventional bargain between a buyer and a seller, plainly does not lend itself to the ordinary checks which are intended to ensure free competition in international trade.

It follows that it is a mistake to suppose that an effective policy for international trade can be achieved by the traditional means of bringing down tariffs and then making sure that the market is not being distorted by unfair practices, like dumping. Quite different and more elaborate rules involving intimate collaboration between countries on such matters as company law and the supervision of intra-company transactions, legislation on health and also on certain minimum social standards are required. Looking ahead, social standards will become more important as the rising share of services in the national product of all advanced countries comes to be reflected in international trade. The traditional checks on unfair trade practices, on discrimination, dumping and so on, are hardly practicable for much of international trade in services.

Moreover, large scale commercial investment nowadays so often

becomes an issue which involves public policy. The decision
whether to go ahead with some venture in a new and risky form of
production turns on obtaining a certain measure of public support, either by direct subsidy or in the form of assured sales out-
lets. That happens most commonly in some of the high technology
industries, like aerospace and computers. The fact that a big international firm with a high reputation is already established in the
market for such products often makes it extremely difficult for a
newcomer to begin to compete. Now it so happens that in Europe
it is the American companies with a proved capacity for high
technology which are most firmly established in a number of
advanced industries. If their dominance is to be challenged – and
there does seem to be a widespread desire in Europe to do so – it
is unlikely that it will be done without a concerted European
effort, involving some financial support from governments, as well
as official discrimination in favour of European industries.

It is here that the problem emerges sharply of accommodating
traditional ideas about the conduct of international trade, which
continue to guide American thinking on the subject, with the
realities of politico-economic competition as the Europeans see
them – most especially when the Europeans feel that they are at a
permanent disadvantage simply because they are latecomers in
some of the most important fields of advanced industrial technology. The analogy that comes to mind is with Germany in the
early nineteenth century faced by the entrenched competitive
power of Britain in export markets across the world. Friedrich
List,[4] the German economist who most vigorously supported the
Zollverein,[5] called on his countrymen at the time to set their faces
against the intellectual blandishments of British propaganda
for world-wide free trade. It was natural, he said, that a nation
like Britain which had all the established market advantages
would claim that straightforward competitive power ought to be
the sole criterion of economic policy. It wanted market forces to
be the sole judge. But unless the Germans protected themselves,
List argued, they would never undertake the investments which
would allow them in the long run to compete with the British on

4. 1789–1846; author of *The National System of Political Economy*.
5. German customs union formed under Prussian auspices.

equal terms. In the present case, the European sentiment against their American competitors is likely to be even stronger, since it is precisely in those industries which have a clear relationship to political power – whether it is telecommunications by satellite or aerospace or computer technology – that American dominance is most marked.

There is thus immense scope for mutual misunderstanding – even without the particular irritant to the Americans of the Community's common agricultural policy. The latter is generally agreed to be an unsatisfactory policy; the Europeans are unhappy with it as well as the Americans. But what must be said about it is that it was an attempt, however ham-fisted, to deal with a serious welfare problem affecting the European farming population. The farmers were, and are, notably poorer than European industrial workers, and to argue that the problem should be left to the free play of market forces to get them off the land and into industry is no help at all. For one thing, they have been moving off the land in massive numbers. From 1950 to 1970 the number of farm workers in the European Community dropped from some twenty million to ten million. It is hard to believe that the decline could have been very much faster without causing acute distress to a lot of people.

There is the further point that in any negotiation about international trade in agricultural produce between Europe and the United States, the Europeans will be saying to the Americans that they cannot bargain about the problem effectively unless both are willing to treat their internal arrangements for propping up agriculture and subsidizing the farm population as matters in which the other side has a legitimate interest. The Community's whole approach to this kind of problem is based on the assumption that if one is seriously trying to reduce the obstacles to freedom of movement of goods, money and persons, one has to be prepared to negotiate with outsiders about a host of subjects which are traditionally thought of as belonging solely to the sphere of domestic policies. Do you really wish to bargain about trade in agricultural produce? – they say to the United States – in that case you must accept that non-Americans will be telling you about the limits on the money you can spend to protect your poor farmers in West

Virginia or on bribing your excessively productive farmers in the Middle West to take some of their land out of cultivation. This is essentially what I mean by the 'Community method'. It is not something which has so far had any attraction for the United States.

In the 1920s President Coolidge said: 'The business of the United States is business'. He summed up an important strand in American thinking – that governments do best when they simply provide the opportunity for the forces of private commerce to assert themselves. By the same token one might say : 'The business of the European Community is politics and social welfare'. Again the Americans, who tend to see this European venture as an exercise in classic New World federalism, designed to liberate the forces of private enterprise from the interference of national states, are going to be disappointed. For this is a very interventionist Community, most active in regulating the domestic affairs of its member countries. At the same time it is annoyingly deficient in clearcut authority when it comes to conducting its relations with outsiders. From an American viewpoint this looks like a nasty combination of busybodying at home and sloth abroad.

Conflict over the Dollar

The new American political tactics, as they have emerged in the 1970s, appear to be an attempt to blackmail the Europeans into creating the collective authority which they lack by presenting them with the threat of massive inaction by the United States. The theory is that once the Europeans realize that the leadership and initiative are no longer coming from the Americans, they will produce some leadership of their own. This approach was much in evidence during the dollar crisis of the latter part of 1971 and afterwards. The Europeans are being told in effect that they must either put up their own substitute for the dollar system – or shut up, and accept the monetary arrangements that are designed to meet American convenience. I suspect that this ploy may have long-term consequences that the Americans may find by no means convenient. It is always risky to invite a number of people to look for a means of agreeing among themselves by ganging up against you. They may, after all, find one! The Europeans are genuinely irked by certain aspects of the American dominance of the world monetary system, and I believe that they could make their own financial arrangements much less dependent on the dollar, while stopping well short of the creation of a fully fledged European monetary union.

The argument is a little technical, but the main point is that the countries of the European Community might agree on a limited number of restrictive rules designed to control certain transactions in dollars and to reduce the use of dollars as part of their currency reserves. In that case they would in effect reduce the freedom of manoeuvre of all dollar-holders; and most of these are still Americans. They might also put the American Treasury in an awkward position if they decided that henceforth the dollar was no longer an acceptable asset to go into their currency reserves. There are already vast quantities of spare dollars in the hands of European central banks, and it is to be expected that they will try to reduce the amount and to agree on common rules restricting the future acquisition of dollars. We in Britain have some experience, through our attempts to deal with the problem of the wartime accumulation of sterling balances, of how a nation's freedom of manoeuvre may be constrained by the need to satisfy the foreign holders of its currency, especially at times when its own balance of payments is under pressure.

Once again there is here a built-in formula for feeding the fires of mutual resentment. For the Americans undoubtedly believe that offering the world the opportunity of converting itself to a dollar currency standard was a great service performed at considerable sacrifice to themselves. They emphasize the fact that in the course of it they lost control over their own currency, because so many other people outside the United States were using it. The Europeans do not deny this fact, but emphasize the very large financial advantages which the Americans have had in the process. The question however is not who is right, but how to find some means of mitigating the quarrel. What is clear is that the recent American tactic of treating it as if it were someone else's problem is not a very promising approach to this objective.

The Nixon–Kissinger Doctrine

One can understand the American aim better if one sees it as part of a more general realignment of policies in the context of what may be called the Nixon–Kissinger doctrine. This is the view that by the late 1960s the American posture in world affairs was both excessively exposed and excessively rigid. The most spectacular moves designed to reduce both exposure and rigidity have concentrated on the United States' enemies, China and Russia. But the allies have also been subjected to an effort to reformulate the terms of their bargain with the United States in such a way as to limit the degree of American involvement. The United States view tends to be that its bargaining position has been weakened, because its allies have been able to exploit the fact that the Americans have such a large stake in the maintenance of the international system itself. There is a branch of game theory applied to international relations which shows how it is that smaller nations have much more freedom to pursue their own national interests than a great power which is concerned above all to preserve and strengthen the system and its rules. American thinking and writing on this somewhat abstract theme suggests that it is a serious preoccupation. It is almost as if the United States Government felt that it too had to demonstrate every now and then that it could play hookey!

My point is that in practice the United States can't. It has too much at stake in the world economic and financial system to opt out. But equally it is not inclined towards the alternative approach, which I have called the 'Community method', because that involves too great a departure from old-established habits of conducting international relations. It is the complete opposite of opting out; indeed it commits you to opt *into* a bargaining process with a lot of foreigners on almost every subject of domestic interest. It would demand radical changes of attitudes – for example, that the Americans should accept as of right a European Community presence in certain phases of their legislative process on Capitol Hill, in parallel with corresponding American rights, exercised perhaps by Committees of the United States Congress,

in Brussels. One would have to be very sanguine to envisage anything more than the most tentative experimental approach to new
political arrangements of this kind for some time yet. In the
meanwhile, the likelihood is that the United States will grow
increasingly impatient with the lack of European leadership, and
that the logic of the slow and laborious process of European integration will produce a rich crop of European bargains that in
one way or another hurt United States interests.

At the back of all this is the awkward but inescapable fact that
the two regions facing each other across the Atlantic are not only
the most developed economically and the most practised in the
sophisticated techniques of representative democracy; they are also
the most pluralistic societies. To make a significant decision in
either of them requires an extensive and complicated process of
internal bargaining with powerful interest groups, as well as the
backing of widespread skills in achieving workable compromises.
The upshot tends to be that when the domestic compromises have
been fixed up and it becomes necessary to move on to a further
stage of negotiating with an outsider, each side finds its position
has already acquired a high degree of rigidity.

No doubt this is considerably worse for the European Community, whose member states are only gradually getting to understand each other and to learn the techniques of effective
compromise. But it would be wrong to underestimate the profound difficulty which a pluralistic society like the United States,
with lots of pressure groups and an open democratic process,
experiences in bargaining abroad about matters involving domestic interests. And this suggests the conclusion that even if the
Europeans were ever to appoint a President and an executive
branch of government, like the Americans, they would still be an
awkward lot to bargain with.

4
Turning Away from Eurafrica

This chapter continues the examination of the external relations of the European Community, focusing mainly on Asia and the Soviet bloc. In Asia the most urgent problem for the Community is probably Japan.

The Japanese are, apart from the Americans, the only major industrial nation in the non-communist world which is not in the enlarged Community. Being more dependent on foreign trade than the United States, Japan is likely to feel the element of discrimination which is built into the Community system even more keenly. Being less important as a market for Europe, also much less significant as a financial power, and, finally, having no military relationship with Europe, its bargaining position is much weaker than that of the Americans. Indeed so far it has been the Americans who have been chiefly instrumental in reminding the Europeans that they have some obligations towards Japan.

The European Community's illusion of living in a private world of its own, while the international system was something which others, notably the Americans, were supposed to look after, was especially noticeable in its attitude towards Japan. Of late, the Americans have been telling the Europeans more and more insistently that Japan – and by that they mean Japanese export trade – is another burden which they will no longer carry alone. The Community, they insist, must recognize that it has a duty to make its contribution.

Part of the trouble has been that the nature of Europe's obligation in this matter has been obscured by Japan's membership of the American system of alliances. Western Europe is also part of that system, but that does not of itself create a working relationship between the two. The Americans have adopted towards the

Japanese very much of a tutelary role, and the Europeans have been more than content to let it be so. There is still a characteristic imperial tone used by the Americans in their dealings with Japan which helps to encourage such an attitude on the European side. Consider as an example the following from President Nixon's Foreign Policy Review for the year 1971: 'We intend that Japan shall remain our most important Asian ally . . . These are the convictions that led me to travel to Alaska to welcome to American soil the Emperor and Empress of Japan on the first visit abroad of a reigning Japanese monarch.' It is not offensive; it just puts the United States in an entirely different class from the rest of us.

This is perhaps one of the reasons why the Europeans do not respond readily to exhortations such as that made in another Presidential report – on international economic policy – that they should import more from Japan, on the ground that almost one third of American imports were Japanese goods, while in the European case they were only 3 per cent.[1] More fundamentally, this kind of statistical comparison seems to reflect a lack of feeling for the impact of foreign trade on economies of the European type. Because the Americans rely on imports for only a tiny part of all that they consume, the economic effect of even a large increase in the proportion of imports from Japan is not very great. One third of total imports is the equivalent of only a little over 1 per cent of the national product of the United States. But for the countries of Western Europe import trade is vastly more important. If the European Community took one third of its imports from Japan that would mean that the equivalent of some 5 per cent of the total output of the EEC would be taken over by Japanese goods. This would pose a problem of adjustment on a heroic scale.

The Need to Accommodate Japan

In general, the problems faced by societies which are highly permeable to external economic forces in adjusting to Japanese competition in world markets are different from anything within the

1. See Peter G. Peterson, *The United States in the Changing World Economy*, 1971.

experience of the United States. One of the key elements in the philosophy underlying the Community is that foreign trade is too important a factor in the economic life of modern European nations to be treated as a fit subject for international bargaining on its own; it needs to be looked at in the context of the overall management of economic and social affairs by a group of like-minded countries. This is their form of re-insurance. But that is not to say that the highly restrictive trade policies which individual West European countries have adopted towards Japan should be continued on a collective basis in the future, when they will have to agree on a single standard set of Community rules applied to all Japanese imports. The Community has obligations to Japan as a highly efficient fellow member of the international trading system. It cannot opt out of these without risking a great deal more than the loss of Japanese economic goodwill.

Japan's wealth and dynamism, its great capacity for organized effort and its skills in advanced technologies ensure that the Japanese will be a major force in world affairs during the rest of this century. Japan will not necessarily be a world power in the old-fashioned sense that it will have command of vast military forces in being; what is important is its future capacity, derived from its extraordinary productive potential, to choose freely among a number of options, of which the military is one. It is, besides, so placed geographically that the choice that it eventually makes must inevitably exercise a profound influence on the whole of Asia; and this is where more than half the world's population lives. To put the matter in stark terms, it is in Western Europe's interest just as much as the United States' that Japan should not feel isolated and so much at variance with the other centres of power in the international system that it is seriously tempted to discard the Western alliance and build its own nuclear weapons. For if the Japanese did decide that they wanted to do this, it is hard to see how they could be stopped.

Short of nuclear weapons, there are the dangers of Japanese reactions to a break-up of the world-wide economic and financial system. If it became apparent that the system was being fragmented into a number of more or less autonomous blocs of countries – a West European bloc, a United States dollar bloc, each with its own collection of satellites, plus the existing Soviet bloc – then the Japanese could hardly refrain from trying to establish a comparable organization of their own, based in Asia and possibly with offshoots in Africa. It is very doubtful whether we would be happier with a Japan which felt that it had been driven into a corner and needed to mobilize all its resources, political as well as economic, in order to organize its survival against the hostility of the Western world.

Yet it has to be recognized on the other side that the European Community faces certain special problems at the present stage in managing its external economic relations with a major industrial power, like Japan. It is not only the fact which was noted in the last chapter, that some of the important bargains among members of the European club tend to be made at the expense of outsiders, most especially if insiders and outsiders have directly competing interests. There is also the less obvious influence exercised by the knowledge that the making of an organization like the European Community represents an implicit commitment on the part of its member states to accept a more rapid and radical change in their social and economic environment than before. They know that giving free play to the movement of goods, people and money within the group makes it inevitable that there will be major alterations in the social landscape of Europe ten or twenty years hence. That is why the more vulnerable countries are so anxious to build in safeguards and insurances which will make the actual process of change less painful and which, more significantly, make it clear from the start that the costs of adjustment to the accelerated pace of change are to be treated as a collective burden to be borne by the Community as a whole. In this situation the Japanese industrial phenomenon looks like a further demand for even more rapid change and adjustment, with far fewer safeguards.

It is no use arguing that having already accepted a much accelerated rate of change – reflecting in effect Europe's decision to make a positive and collective response to the second industrial revolution – the Europeans should not baulk at this additional demand for industrial adaptation. For the fact is that what I have called the 'Community method' is a particular style of adaptation. It is a style that can only be practised effectively by a group of nations at a very similar level of economic development, with common social and political objectives, and a ready means of understanding each other and coping with national variations.

Some of the arguments which suggested that the United States was a very doubtful practitioner of the 'Community method' seem to apply with even greater force to Japan. True, the Japanese feel altogether more exposed and vulnerable than the United States. But there is one condition which it would be especially difficult for Japan to fulfil: that is to establish a society which is in practice as permeable to outside pressures and influences as the West European countries are today. There are, besides, quite exceptional problems of adaptation that will have to be faced by the Japanese, working in the context of a highly traditionalist society – especially so in regard to the structure of authority – and of a fantastic pace of economic advance, which causes changes in the conditions of living that are normally spread over a generation to be squeezed into less than a decade.

These factors, taken together, as well as others like the keen Japanese sense of separate national identity, would make it extremely difficult to arrive at those wide-ranging bargains on domestic affairs, involving common solutions to common social and economic problems, which are the characteristic stuff of the European Community. One alternative is the method used by the Americans to deal with the domestic difficulties caused by excessive Japanese competitive power. They concede the general principle of most-favoured-nation treatment for all Japanese goods, give them a free run of the market on equal terms with other countries; but then blackmail the Japanese into imposing so-called 'voluntary' export restrictions on their own exports of products like textiles and steel, in an effort to limit the damage done to particular American industries. This seems to be a way of maximizing the resentment on both sides. What is lacking is any principle of reciprocity, leading to a fair exchange of benefits, as well as of restrictions. Japan too has social and political problems which are aggravated by the pressures coming from its trading partners. Where the European Community might make a distinctive contribution would be in approaching these matters as joint problems, to be tackled jointly. It will not be easy, but a start has to be made somewhere in treating Japan's domestic economic problems as matters of normal international concern.

The EEC and the Underdeveloped Countries

By contrast the European Community's relations with the poor underdeveloped majority in Asia, outside the islands of Japan, lend themselves to more straightforward measures. This aspect of European policy has been given a curious archaic twist because of the particular time and incidental circumstances of the signing of the Treaty of Rome. One has to remember that at that time, in the late 1950s, France was in the final stages of its last colonial war, in Algeria, that the other Mediterranean countries which France had ruled were still regarded as permanent client states of the French, and that in Black Africa the French were determined to hang on to everything they had. Belgium was obsessed by its interests in the Congo, and the Italians too were concerned to retain their special position in Somalia. Fifteen years later the theory and the procedures of the European Community are still influenced by those out-of-date notions – in particular by the idea of Eurafrica and of the Mediterranean as a European lake, in which neither the United States nor Russia have any business to be in the long run. If one thinks of a British parallel, it is as if our policies towards the Third World today were still guided by the objectives of the late 1950s, when much of Africa was still ruled from Whitehall and when it was thought to be absolutely vital that Britain should maintain its colonial position in the military bases of Singapore, Aden and Cyprus.

The result of the Community's geographical obsession with the area to the south of it has been that the interests of the Asians, and most particularly of the Indian sub-continent, have hardly figured at all in its policies towards the underdeveloped world. However, in the meanwhile within the Community itself there has been a gradual shift in the balance of economic power – a shift from south to north reflected in the economic ascendancy of Germany – which has had its counterpart in the actual distribution of European aid. The Germans give more economic aid to India than to any other nation; so does Britain. With the entry of the three new

North European members of the Community it is a safe bet that the re-orientation of the Community away from the development of a southern satellite region will continue. One has to remember that it was at one stage very much an open question whether the EEC would become a Mediterranean-centred group, as France desired, with some northern appendages – or whether, as has now happened, its centre of gravity would shift decisively northwards. General de Gaulle never concealed his preference for Spain over Britain as a potential partner in the Community.

It is not only the original geographical choice made by the Community but also the institutional form of its policies towards underdeveloped countries which have caused a certain distortion. It has negotiated a series of so-called 'association agreements', by which a number of countries are able to claim privileges in trade, and also sometimes in aid, as Associated States of the Community. The very language reflects the underlying notion of a relatively weak client state being granted certain privileges derived from a special historical relationship with a more powerful metropolitan centre. It was intended for the relatively underdeveloped countries of Southern Europe and the Mediterranean and for former colonies in Africa. When the British presented the case of their former possessions in the Indian sub-continent, no one even contemplated offering them an 'association agreement'. And because the EEC seemed to have nothing much else to offer, the Indian Ocean got left out. Over the long run that has had the further consequence, which has been bad for the political development of the Community itself, that the big issues of policy towards the Third World have had to be tackled by member countries individually and not as a common endeavour.

Perhaps the arrival of Britain really will make a difference in this case. Certainly it is the hope of some senior officials in Brussels, who think that reform is overdue, that British membership will widen the horizons of Community development policy. At present there is still the traditional concern with an exchange of trading privileges which is the basis of the 'association agreements': the underdeveloped country concerned is given access on favourable terms to the market of the Community for certain of its products, and in return is expected to grant preferential treatment to the products of the Community. (The exception to this rule is the limited 'general preference' for exports from all the underdeveloped countries, which has now been conceded in principle by all the industrial nations.) In practice the results of these preferential arrangements are extremely provocative to those, like the United States, who are discriminated against; and the total value of the additional trade thus gained by the Community is not really big enough to be worth fighting about.

It is not clear, however, that the EEC is seriously looking for economic advantage; the whole business seems rather to be the confused expression of a general principle that has somehow become embedded in the Community's conduct of its international relations. It starts by wanting to have an active international policy in the traditional sense. But if its favours to particular nations are not to be distributed on the basis of some principle of reciprocity, reflecting a set of continuing relationships between the partners to the act, then it would be hard to find a basis for choosing to cultivate any one country rather than another. It would follow that the Community would have to distribute its assistance to developing countries, whether in the form of financial aid or commercial favours, in accordance with a general rule applicable equally to all comers. It would not be able to discriminate.

'Civilian Power'

In my view this is precisely the approach which is appropriate for the European Community of the 1970s. There is a great deal of self-criticism by officials of the EEC of their own development policies – they are felt by many in Brussels to be thoroughly inadequate – and among the most vociferous critics in Sicco Mansholt, the President of the European Commission in 1972. However, it is doubtful whether the Community will in practice be able to achieve the results that it wants in this field unless it discards some of the underlying political assumptions which continue to provide the ideological framework for its policies. Chief of these is the notion, which powerfully influenced the origins of the European Community, that it would conduct its external relations as if it were a kind of super-state in embryo, systematically building up friendships with selected countries and not with others. Given that this was the theory, it was entirely logical that the Community should construct a network of preferential trade agreements, which now cause so much anger in the United States and elsewhere. Unlike the United States or any other nation, the Community's capacity to function as if it were a government of six countries was effectively confined to the management of trade. If it wanted some client-state relationships, this was the only instrument to hand.

But why should it try to cultivate such relationships, since it is clear that it neither is nor will become a super-state? It acts, for example in the Mediterranean, almost as if it was another great power which might one day be asking the nations along the coasts which receive its commercial favours for base facilities for a Community navy! If any of the individual members of the Community do indeed want arrangements of this kind, then it is up to them, using their own resources, to make the appropriate bargains. The EEC's external relations would then be liberated from a certain geographical parochialism, and it would be able to make its distinctive contribution, as a Community, to international relations. The fact that it is not a super-state, that it is not dominated by old-fashioned notions of sovereignty but manages a network of wide-ranging common activities which transcend the narrow political environment of the nation state, endows it with certain positive advantages in the conduct of some aspects of international relations. Nationhood can be very inhibiting; there are all sorts of assumptions and postures adopted by the representatives of nations which constrict their room for manoeuvre.

We should not, however, underestimate the spiritual adjustment that will have to be made if the Community is to rid itself entirely of its geographical inhibitions. It is after all located in Europe and designed to serve Europeans. Characteristically, once it was clear that Britain was joining the Community, leaving EFTA[2] without its main market, Brussels set about negotiating a new and bigger European free-trade area to look after the threatened interests of Britain's previous EFTA partners. This was formed in 1972. France then promptly proposed that the same principle ought to be applied to the large group of countries in

2. The European Free Trade Association, formed in 1960.

the Mediterranean area, some European and some not, which had made special agreements with the Community. It seemed to have a certain logic – and so here one was, back again with the old French vision of a Mediterranean centre of gravity, the Latins to balance the northern intruders, and ultimately of a union of Eurafrica. The honest answer to the French on this matter is that the EFTA countries of the north and centre of Europe which are outside the Community – Sweden, Norway, Finland, Switzerland and Austria – are a different case: they are all advanced industrial societies with high living standards, developed social welfare systems, and liberal arrangements governing the relationship between the state and its citizens. The Community can readily arrive at common decisions with them on the basis of common assumptions covering a wide range of social and economic policy. (Portugal, the one south European member of EFTA, is a different case; but then it was always treated as different and special inside EFTA too.)

It would, I believe, help the Community to be more effective if it recognized openly that it is a rich man's club – European, because the experience of growing up in Europe has contributed so much to the similarity of the social and economic problems of this group of affluent societies. Acknowledging the material advantage on which the Community is founded would not be a reason for being less generous in their dealings with poorer countries. It would simply make for more realism in devising the appropriate form for the relationship and in choosing the means, whether through aid or trade, which are most likely to contribute to the process of economic development. Indeed, the formulation of a common development policy towards the Third World offers an especially promising field for the further progress of European integration (see Chapter 6). It is a field in which the conventional assumptions of Western nation-states about old-style power relationships based on gifts and favours urgently need to be discarded. The Community – which is the purest expression in the international system of what François Duchene has called 'civilian power', as opposed to traditional military/political power – is exceptionally well placed to demonstrate how to do it.

The third area which I want to discuss in this abbreviated survey of the Community's external relations is Eastern Europe. Here the Community has so far been hampered by the relentless hostility of the Soviet Union. The Soviet Government has refused to have any official dealings with it, and the other East European countries have perforce fallen into line. The EEC has continued to be treated as if it were nothing more than an instrument of the cold war – a device, like NATO, invented by the Americans to mobilize the West European nations in a united front against the East. There is of course no denying that at the outset, during the 1950s, the fear of Soviet Russia and of its possible alliance with powerful local communist parties in a highly vulnerable area of Europe was a strong motive force for the construction of the European Community. One has to recall just how exposed this whole area appeared to be at the time – with the West Germans an unknown political quantity, able to provide no assurance about how they would respond to constant Russian pressure along their eastern borders, while in two other important nations of the Six, France and Italy, powerful communist parties and their allies were polling a quarter or more of the total votes and dominating the trade unions. Here in these three nations were 150 million people who looked as if they were seriously at risk; acting together they would stand a better chance of survival. It was indeed a function of the Community, which the Soviets especially resented, to provide the international framework within which Western Germany's political resurgence as a major European power was consolidated. But the curious thing is that the Russians continued to treat the EEC as the pliant instrument of American international policies long after it became clear in the course of the 1960s that there was growing friction between the two.

It is not to be supposed, however, that the Russians will continue indefinitely trying to warm themselves over the cold embers of extinct ideological fires. The enlargement of the Community to include virtually all the advanced nations of Western Europe which are not neutrals will surely provide an occasion for some rethinking in Moscow. The refusal of the formal act of recognition has so far been a nuisance only to some of the small East European countries, which have had to conduct their discussions with the Community on certain trade matters which are vitally important to them as if they were not really happening. It has put them at a disadvantage in negotiation. Moscow's dislike for the Common Market is no doubt partly due to the fact that it so much prefers the traditional method of dealing with Western nations singly, and if possible in competition with one another, rather than collectively. But now that the members of the European Community are firmly committed to begin to move, from 1973 onwards, to a new system for the joint conduct of their commercial relations with the rest of the world, the old type of bilateral trade agreements which the Russians have used to conduct their economic relations with the individual countries of Western Europe for the past forty or fifty years will no longer be feasible.

Paradoxically, some of the East European communist countries fear this development precisely because they think that it may well have the effect of strengthening the Russian grip on the management of their relations with the West. So long as the West European countries were negotiating with them individually, each East European state was able to set up its own network of bilateral trading and financial arrangements. But if there is in future to be one negotiation on behalf of all the nine countries of the Community, it will be hard to resist the pressure for a collective Soviet-bloc response. Hitherto the Comecon, Eastern Europe's trade organization, has concerned itself exclusively with the internal transactions among members of the bloc. The Russians are naturally, if only because of the sheer size of their economy compared with those of the other communist countries, overwhelmingly dominant in Comecon. It would be highly unwelcome if they came to dominate in the same way the growing network of trade relations between Western Europe and such countries as Hungary, Poland and East Germany. The East Germans would be a particularly tricky case, since there is a special protocol of the Treaty of Rome which gives them, alone among the members of the Soviet bloc, duty-free access for their exports to the European Common Market via West Germany.

It is not only that these East European countries prefer to run their own business with the West rather than have another country, especially one so powerful as the Soviet Union, taking a hand in a collective negotiation. There is also the fundamental economic fact that the Russians are not deeply committed international traders. Importing and exporting for them are very marginal activities; their foreign trade absorbs at most 2 to 3 per cent of their national product. Compare this with a country like Hungary where foreign trade accounts for more than a third. The Hungarians know that if they are to survive they have to persuade foreigners to buy a very large part of all that they produce – and that if they are to progress, they must make sure that the amount which they manage to sell abroad increases substantially each year. Hungary is the extreme case, but the other industrialized countries of Eastern Europe – Czechoslovakia, East Germany and Poland – share the same anxiety about foreign markets. This is not a small matter in determining the style of a nation. The Russian leaders know, or believe they know, that in the last resort they would be able to fall back on the resources of their own country and survive, even if other nations refused to do business with them. The Hungarians and the others know that they are condemned to be active members of the international economic system.

Moreover they are convinced that if they are to succeed as international traders, increasing their exports from year to year, they must be able to sell sophisticated industrial products of the most advanced design. They are therefore determined not only to maintain close scientific contacts with the West, but also more and more to involve Western enterprise and capital in their own industrial ventures. Partnership in production and management is believed to be the key to marketing industrial products in the West.

It is to be observed that this approach to selling by way of a partnership in production contrasts markedly with traditional notions of capitalist economics, which treat marketing as a discrete operation, guided by the principles of free competition towards an optimum price. It is of course very much in line with communist ideas about the relationship between production and distribution. The East Europeans want partners in the West because they believe that selling without the backing of a close and continuing economic relationship is unlikely to be successful. So there is an element of paradox here. They want to run their own exclusive national plans, but they want to build foreign enterprise closely into the process of production. They can only do that of course if the plans of the capitalist foreigner and those of the East European government fit together. It may not yet have struck the planners on the other side, but the logic of the 'industrial cooperation agreement', the favourite device for bringing Western enterprise into East European trade, leads to some degree of joint decision-making about East European production and economic policy. The more successful and widespread the joint enterprises are, the more significant this factor becomes. Again, for the Russians the issue is marginal. But for the smaller East European countries, which depend much more on foreign trade and on imported technology, the repercussions of successful business collaboration with firms in the West could be considerable.

Add to this an important development in industrial management which has begun to appear in a number of East European countries. Hungary will again serve as an illustration, because it has led in the effort to get away from the centralization of management decisions and to make more use of the independent initiatives of managers of individual enterprises. They are being encouraged to go out and sell, to run their state-owned enterprises as if they were profit-making businesses, and to that end they have been given more freedom to make direct business arrangements with firms in the West. The practice of direct collaboration between communist and Western capitalist enterprises is still at an early stage, but the acceptance of the principle is itself of some significance. It is potentially another element in the system of transnational relationships – that is, the arrangements between organizations and groups located in different countries which by-pass the central government – which I have argued are characteristic of contemporary Western industrial society. The proliferation and variety of these relationships and their increased influence on the way that society is run have provided the essential economic and social environment for the European Community. It is clear that if the East European reformers of the decentralizing school are successful in the sphere of foreign commerce and investment, they will find that they too are involved more and more in transnational relations which tend to develop their own momentum.

The process may well be reinforced in two ways which deserve a brief mention. First of all the European Community tends to think of the states of Eastern Europe, especially those that are closer at hand and have been an integral part of the main strands of European history – Czechoslovakia, East Germany, Hungary and Poland – as countries belonging to the same family as themselves. Legal niceties will not prevent the Community from searching for devices which, when there is a demand from the other side, will give these nations privileged treatment. It is in principle the same case as that of the neutral countries belonging to EFTA: their international political status imposes limitations on the extent of their formal involvement in the Community, but other arrangements are devised to ensure that their economic interests are safeguarded. How to achieve this result in Eastern Europe without appearing to challenge Russia's position of dominance in the area is going to be one of the major problems of the foreign policy of the European Community during the 1970s and 1980s.

There is no doubt that the Russians will be sensitive – among other things, to the extraordinary pull that is still exercised by West European culture on these East European countries. This is the other element in this incipient transnational relationship. After all, the Community contains three nations which have in different ways exerted immensely powerful influences on the minds and attitudes of the modern East European intelligentsia. They are France, Germany and Britain – and they continue to exert an extraordinary spiritual magnetism. This is likely to add to the other strains between Russia and the smaller industrialized members of the Soviet bloc. If, as I have argued, there is some room for manoeuvre in this situation for a Community foreign policy aiming at more autonomy for the East European nations in their dealings with the West, it can only be because in the end the USSR will be deterred from taking the extreme measures which would be necessary in order to maintain strict control over the management of every phase of the life of these countries.

The Soviet Government may of course decide in the end that it is worth re-establishing the regional tyranny of Eastern Europe which existed in the early 1950s. In that case the Community's 'civilian power' will be worthless. But there is at least a fair chance that the EEC may be given an opportunity to demonstrate what an enlightened foreign economic policy, skilfully pursued, can do to make the division between the two parts of Europe progressively less complete and less painful.

I must however conclude this exploration of the international relationships of the enlarged Community, which has occupied the last two chapters, on a note of deeper questioning. What will be the long-term effect on the attitudes of Western Europe itself of the frictions and pressures that are likely to come upon it in the 1970s and 1980s – the replacement of America's active support by a kind of demanding distrust, the suspicion and probable rivalry of Japan, the continued hostility of the Soviet Union even after it has reluctantly conceded formal recognition? More important, the West Europeans will be living in a world in which the big decisions setting the essential military and strategic framework of international relations look like being made in agreement by the two established super-powers, Russia and America, with less participation on the part of America's European allies of today. Europe may become a more anxious place, less secure in its assumptions about the international order in which its room for manoeuvre will have been reduced, and in consequence probably more aggressive in asserting what it recognizes as its own separate interests. It may even be driven more rapidly into political cohesion by the sense of an unfriendly international environment in which its needs will not be readily accorded a high priority. The world of more compact regional blocs which seems to be opening up will not be a comfortable place to live in. This chapter has been mainly about Europe's opportunities; but the big issue may turn out to be how to avoid the mood of 'fortress Europe'.

5
From Technocracy to Democracy?

The last two chapters have identified some pretty large tasks that lie ahead of the European Community, tasks which will demand definite decisions from it. Perhaps the most urgent of them is to sort out a collective position for the nine member states vis-à-vis the Americans on the wide range of questions connected with the reorganization of world trade and money to replace the Bretton Woods system. Yet the Community as it stands is an extremely inefficient instrument for decision-making. Indeed it may have been felt that there was a certain contradiction between the character of this organization as I have described it, growing out of a somewhat amorphous mass of complementary activities of a very varied kind with a central authority wholly dependent upon securing a consensus among its members, and on the other side the series of major decisions that I suggest are required of it. In fact, I take the view that the Community will be able to manage its relations with the rest of the world, with the Soviet bloc, Japan, the underdeveloped countries, as well as with the United States, only if it arrives at a more efficient method of making its decisions. That is the subject of this chapter.

It is a highly contentious subject, for it involves the clash of different philosophies about the essential nature of the Community. It is clear that there are two major defects in the Community's processes. First they are excessively slow; there is no routine for forcing a decision even if a clear majority of the members want it. Secondly, the Brussels organization suffers by comparison with national governments because it does not have the democratic legitimacy possessed by the latter. The matters which are decided in the name of the Community do not command popular obedience based on the feeling that the decisions, even when they are not liked, emanate from a body which is in the last resort sustained by the freely given support of a majority of the population. It is too technocratic. One of the questions which will be brought to a head by Britain's entry is how to begin to shift it from technocracy towards democracy.

The European federalists of the traditional school believe that they have a ready means to hand for solving both problems, that of democratic legitimacy and of more efficient decision-making, at once. The means that they propose is to set up a directly elected European Parliament with the constitutional power to over-ride, in the last resort, the Council of Ministers, who make all the important Community decisions today. It is an attractive idea: you call in the direct voice of the people, transcending national frontiers, and use it to force member governments to act in unison with one another and to face problems that they would prefer to evade. The trouble is that it is not only governments who would have to be flouted and bullied in the process. After all, behind these governments there are the national parliaments and in each of these there is a majority of MPs whose assent to the government's policies is needed to sustain it in power. It is worth noting that the majority is not necessarily enthusiastic or even wholehearted in its support of every one of the government's measures; it is the broad balance of what it does that attracts its support.

Now into this situation we must imagine, in the extreme case, the sudden eruption of a vote by the European Parliament contradicting a decision by one of the national governments. Assume that the government is supported by a majority at home – and what we have is an invitation to a fight between the national parliament and the European Parliament. This would be an extremely dangerous confrontation. Who would say which of the two, the national or the European parliamentary body, had the sounder democratic base in making decisions about the national policies of one of the member states? In practice the great bulk of the day-to-day business of governing the peoples of the Community is, and will be for many years, conducted by the national parliaments. That is where the governments who are responsible for the conduct of this business must look for their support. There is no corresponding function for the European Parliament, for the cogent reason that this is not a federation of states with a central

government but a Community of nations feeling its way forward
to a number of collective decisions. To take just one example – the
whole budget of the Community, over which the European Parliament has recently obtained additional powers of control, amounts
to just about 1 per cent of the combined national products of the
member countries. By contrast, the national budgets of the members commonly involve sums amounting to some 30 to 40 per cent
of their national products. The national parliament is where the
action is; and it will remain there unless the national parliaments
themselves decide on an act of abnegation on a massive scale,
surrendering their power to tax, to spend, and therefore to decide
the fates of governments, to a European Parliament.

National MPs in the European Parliament

I have indicated in earlier chapters why such a development is
highly improbable. Certainly the way to achieve the collaboration
between national parliaments and the European parliamentary
body at the centre, which is an essential condition for the democratic functioning of the EEC, is not to start by organizing a competition in power between them. The reality is that the present
concentration of authority in the Council of Ministers corresponds
to a widespread feeling that a body like this is a necessary safeguard
for certain national interests which may not be shared by other
members of the Community. None of the nations wishes to find
itself in a situation where a European parliamentary majority,
which may not be sensitive to its particular needs, acquires absolute authority to decide these matters. In the Council of Ministers
national representatives cannot be over-ridden in the same way.
And it should not be thought that this approach argues a weak
attachment to the principles of democracy. Countries like Holland
and Germany have shown how their parliaments can keep tabs on
the way in which their ministers comport themselves in the European Council of Ministers. In the last resort, if the members of
these parliaments do not like particular decisions made by their
ministers in the European Community, they can make it very difficult for their national governments to rule effectively; they can
harass them into submission.

Again, we come back to the central fact that until there is a functioning European government, the crucial component of the parliamentary mechanism will be missing.

That is one of the reasons why it is most especially fortunate that the European Community has devised a parliamentary system in which the representatives are drawn from existing MPs of the national parliaments. There is a school of thought among the Europeans in Brussels which constantly laments this fact, as if it was in itself a derogation from a truly 'Communitarian' principle. It seems to me, on the contrary, a thoroughly good thing that the people who are called upon to man the European Parliament have some part in, and experience of, the exercise of real parliamentary power in their home countries. The more the national and the European parliamentarians overlap, arranging their timetables of work jointly, belonging to common parliamentary committees, and using their presence in the two places as a means of putting *additional* pressure on ministers to respond to public opinion, the better.

However, here once more we are up against an obstacle which is deeply embedded in the original ideology of the Community. The European Parliament, alongside the European Commission, was seen as being potentially the pure expression of a European will, quite independent of national will. I have even heard it argued by people in positions of the highest authority in Brussels that the European democratic process would be tainted in some way if, when there are direct elections to the European Parliament, they are held on the same day as elections to the national parliaments. The contagion of national sentiment must, they argue, be prevented at the source!

One becomes very much aware in these European discussions on parliamentary government of the extent to which arguments are influenced by different national experiences of democracy. I had this fact forced upon my attention when I was serving on the Vedel Committee; I was a little puzzled at first to find that the Italians tended to take the most extreme federal line, because they are not notable for national self-abnegation in other matters. But here they seemed to be happily contemplating the prospect of stripping the parliament in Rome of its rights and handing them

over forthwith to the European Parliament in Strasbourg. I was
driven to the conclusion that behind this attitude was the fact
that Italy's experience of parliamentary democracy has been relatively short-lived and most of it not very satisfactory. They might
not feel that they were giving up all that much by comparison
with countries like Holland or Germany. One should remember
in regard to Germany that, leaving the Hitler period aside – that is
a dozen years of its history – it has a long tradition of powerful
opposition politics in parliament, which for instance in Kaiser
Wilhelm's Germany before the First World War sustained a
socialist party bigger than had been seen anywhere before, polling
nearly a third of all the votes. But in Italy's case it is not solely a
matter of parliamentary history. There is the ever present dilemma
of how to govern a country in which the representatives of something close to 40 per cent of the voters, consisting of the communists and their allies on one side and the neo-fascists on the other,
are regarded as permanently excluded from the governmental process. One Italian politician of strong European persuasions put
the point to me succinctly: if, he said, that 40 per cent were
forced to operate in a European parliamentary system comprising
the electorates of the enlarged Community, they would be reduced
to around 10 per cent – which is a relatively small obstacle to
effective government.

On this showing the Italians are looking to an all-powerful
European Parliament to make Italian democracy work. In practice there is no chance that the other countries of the Community,
especially the older democracies in the north of Europe, led by
Britain, would be willing to weaken their own well-established
parliamentary practice in order to deal with the problems of a
malfunctioning democracy in one of their number. Organized
political consent is too precious a national asset to be sacrificed
anyway.

Economic and Monetary Union

How then is the European Community to achieve a much greater
capacity than it has at present for making joint decisions? The
current conventional wisdom of the Community itself on this sub-

ject is that the member nations require the experience of a second bout of the actual process of integration, such as they had during the early years when the Community got rid of its internal tariffs and established a customs union. The new experience of integration that they envisage is the setting up of an Economic and Monetary Union in Western Europe. That is the official line, and all governments have once again, in the autumn of 1972 at the summit meeting in Paris, affirmed this objective.

But behind the apparent unison there is a sharp divergence of views about the steps to be taken to arrive at the desired end. The issue can be stated in its simplest form as follows: in the approach to economic and monetary union, do you start with economic policy or with money? There is no doubt that so far at any rate the Community, largely influenced by French views on the subject, has concentrated its effort overwhelmingly on monetary policy. The first stage is a complicated set of rules about the way in which each of the member countries is to manage its currency, with the gradual result that the central banks of Western Europe would become locked in with one another. As the process continues they are supposed to lose their individual freedom of manoeuvre; the management of national finances, covering such matters as interest rates and the supply of money and credit, which profoundly influence the level of economic activity and of employment, would cease to be determined by each country individually and would be subjected to joint policy decisions made with the concerted authority of the Community. The plan can be characterized as a scheme for European integration by central bankers instead of governments. The hope is evidently that central bankers, being recognized as technicians, will be allowed to get on with their job with the minimum of interference from politicians and the populace at large.

This does not seem to be a promising line of approach to European integration. On the contrary, since existing differences in the monetary policies of the member countries reflect real differences in their economic circumstances, forcing them into a uniform posture on this front without having tackled the fundamental issues of economic policy could well be a formula for aggravating the strains between them. When it comes to the point and a nation is faced with a financial crisis which seriously threatens the well-being of its citizens, it can hardly be expected to treat the management of the exchange rate for its currency as something over which it surrenders control. That was certainly the view taken by Britain when it was faced with a sudden run on the pound sterling in the summer of 1972. It was also the view taken by the German Government in a crisis of an opposite kind the year before.

Moreover it is worth making the point that to surrender control over these matters to a group of European central bankers acting independently of individual governments would be a retrograde step in political terms. It has been one of the aims of post-war economic policy in many countries to bring the central banks, which in the past have been altogether too independent for the economic comfort of those affected by their actions, under more effective supervision by governments. This move reflected the essential realization that decisions by central banks, however technical their appearance, have profound political consequences and that the implied political choices ought to be right out in the open from the beginning. The politics of monetary union in the Community will surely not be allowed to give the central bankers a licence once again to bypass the politicians. And if it is argued that the scheme does leave room for other national elements besides the central banks to be involved, for example the ministers of finance and their top officials and perhaps trade-union and business representatives, then the objective of a joint European board of management running the currencies of the member countries from day to day and securing the appropriate financial measures at home is lost. We are back with the familiar bargaining process between national interests, professional interests, business interests and the rest, which is characteristic of Community politics to date – the long and patient search for consensus, the putting together of package deals and the compromises that go with them.

As the reader will have noticed, I do not believe there is a way of escaping these; indeed the underlying theme of this book is the Community's need to learn to live with this fact during the period ahead. At the moment it seems to be showing some reluctance to learn. And meanwhile the concentration on such apparent escape hatches as a quick European monetary union is causing damage to the whole enterprise. A scheme like this, which suggests that it only needs the goodwill of the member states to achieve again something of that high performance that was realized in the first phase of the construction of Europe, leads inexorably to recriminations and bitterness among the members, when these expectations break down. Already it has produced an unpleasant atmosphere of moral bullying of Germany by France. The French are the leading exponents of the monetary scheme; the Germans are reluctant. And each time it comes to crisis-point the French adopt the favourite posture of General de Gaulle, staring their opponent between the eyes, threatening breakdown, and demanding whether he is ready to accept responsibility for all the consequences that will follow. So far the Germans have felt unable to resist this blackmail, and they have had to sacrifice one Minister of Economics and Finance, Dr Schiller, in the process.[1]

The circumstances of recent German politics have of course been rather special. Willy Brandt's Coalition Government was primarily concerned to bring to completion its novel and difficult policy of reconciliation with Eastern Europe, and it wanted above all to avoid serious trouble on its Western flank. Besides, it had lost its majority in parliament and could not rely on the support at home that it would have needed in order to conduct a successful quarrel with a determined French Government. France has indeed been remarkably successful so far in making support for the policy of quick monetary union the touchstone of loyalty to the European Community. But I wonder how long this success will endure once Britain, which has obvious reasons for hesitation, adds its weight to that of Germany inside the Community. It is evident that the French are not entirely unworried on that score either.

The Technique of Parallel Legislation

The problem of how to reinforce the Community's capacity for decisive action therefore remains. No doubt, a manifest crisis requiring a joint policy in a hurry would be a good help – a military threat or the prospect of a world slump or perhaps some criti-

1. He resigned from Brandt's Coalition Government in summer 1972 after a cabinet crisis – for a combination of reasons of which this was one.

cal shortage of a commodity like oil putting our whole economic system at risk. I think it is a reasonable probability that we shall face a crisis either of this kind or another during the next couple of decades. But we cannot rely on it for the construction of a European political system. What we can do now is to design our institutions with such a prospect in mind – so that they will have the capacity to respond without long delays to critical situations.

Given this objective, there are, it seems to me, two ideas that are especially worth attention. Both are very unglamorous. One is legitimacy; the other is habit. I have already said something about the need to demonstrate as explicitly as possible that the decisions taken by the Community are firmly grounded in the democratic process to which its member states are accustomed. This kind of legitimacy involves much more than the use of a ballot box. It is the quality of the parliamentary process which follows on elections that matters: that process must at the very least be open, accessible to the public and uninhibited. I shall return to this subject later. But first I want to say something about the other factor – the influence of habit.

There is the specific influence that could be exerted on the working methods of the Community by the habit of solving together problems posed by divergent laws and practices in the member states. The issues involved are individually often not of the highest importance. But cumulatively they do add up to something significant. How do you set about reaching basic agreement on common rules for coping with some matter like safety at work or avoiding industrial pollution? You want to make sure that you have got rid of as many differences in these rules as possible and that the inconveniences caused by those which remain are reduced to a minimum; that is the essential aim of the Community exercise – to eliminate any practice which allows the nationals of one member country to discriminate against those of another. They may not consciously wish to discriminate; they may simply be obeying rules of behaviour that happen to have been adopted for purely local reasons in the past. They would be quite willing to change these rules in order to make them less inconvenient to the outsider, if he were prepared to do the same for them. Both would benefit in the end from there being one set of rules governing transactions and activities in which they are equally involved. The European Community has found that there is a vast amount of work to be done on the harmonization of national laws, far more than was originally anticipated.

It has been argued, I think very persuasively, by Professor Kahn-Freund[2] that this work could be better done if there were less emphasis on the exercise of formal legislative power by the Community and more reliance were placed on informal agreements among the legislators in the different national parliaments. He points in particular to the experience of the United States in arriving at broadly uniform Federal laws by this means – that is by inducing the State Legislatures to vote certain uniform laws into existence, affecting virtually all American citizens, without involving the Congress of the United States in any way. This is potentially an important device in the European context and is worth examining further.

The United States Commissioners on Uniform State Laws are an independent body of lawyers who set themselves up in the 1890s in order to deal with some of the inconveniences caused by legal variations in different parts of American territory.[3] At a time of immensely rapid economic expansion, when the United States was establishing its position as the leading industrial nation of the world, arbitrary differences in legal rights and obligations between one state and another could be a serious nuisance. Now although the Commissioners are an unofficial organization, they include in practice the chief law officers of all the states. They work out of the limelight, take copious evidence from the interest-groups affected by their proposals, and secure the cooperation of the legal profession in drafting laws of high technical quality. These 'model laws' are then presented to individual State Legislatures on the independent initiative of elected representatives and senators.

A noteworthy feature of this process is that the object is not to achieve total standardization. The main thing is that any variations in the law which a state wishes to introduce should be a

2. See his lecture, *European Community Law and the British Legal System*, Civil Service College, 7 February 1972.

3. See W. D. Malcolm, 'The Uniform Commercial Code in the United States', *International and Comparative Law Quarterly*, January 1963.

matter of conscious decision by its legislators and not made frivolously or by accident. Secondly such variations should not affect a point of substance or principle; the ample literature surrounding the texts of the model acts put out by the United States Commissioners ensures that there is no misunderstanding on this matter. Thirdly the Commissioners themselves have a regular system for monitoring the variations on the 'model laws' as they are introduced by individual states; so that everyone knows exactly how far they have got in the process of harmonization, and the pressure to go forward is maintained.

It is interesting to find – this is another point made by Professor Kahn-Freund – that a similar process of achieving uniform legislation by the independent action of individual states went forward in Germany in the middle years of the last century during the period preceding the creation of the unified German Reich in 1871. The German states found it imperative at that stage to adopt a common commercial code if they were to develop their trade effectively within the customs union which they had created; and by the early 1860s the job was substantially done. This is a suggestive historical analogy for the European Community, which also has a customs union as its foundation stone.

Indeed, the habit of parallel legislation by the national parliaments of Europe could turn out to be an exceptionally powerful agent of European integration. Kahn-Freund goes as far as to predict that the Community organs as such will tend to play a diminished role as legislators, and that the European Commission in particular will come to have the role of 'technical expert and honest broker' helping the drafters of laws in the member states to arrive at understandings with each other, out of which a new corpus of European law will gradually emerge. It is worth adding that the very nature of the European Community, with its base embedded in the transnational interest-groups, makes this method of moving forward especially appropriate. For these interest-groups are accustomed to the techniques of parallel action in the different countries where their membership is located, and their organizations are in many cases especially skilled in the necessary political techniques. A method of this kind might be expected to have a special appeal for Britain, where there is a highly developed national cult of using the informal and the non-governmental to shape the political environment. However, the European Commission would have to live down its pronounced centralizing tradition, if it were to adapt itself to a method such as this; its preference hitherto has been strongly for total uniformity and for legislative enactment from above. It was indeed part of the federalist doctrine of the early stages of the Community that these two conditions had to be met if Europe's foundations were to be secure; and this particular doctrine is still very much alive in Brussels.

Democratic Legitimacy

That brings the argument back to the issue of democratic legitimacy and the need to strengthen the visible links between what happens at the European centre and public opinion in the member countries. Hitherto one of the troubles with the European Parliament in Strasbourg has been that it has regarded itself as being simply a lobby for Europe, and in particular for the European Commission. To adapt Lloyd George's phrase about the House of Lords which Mr Balfour dominated in the 1900s, the European Parliament has tended to behave like 'Mr Mansholt's poodle'.

The truth is that a parliament which does not engage intermittently in a knockdown fight with a bureaucracy – however wise, however efficient that bureaucracy may be – becomes spiritless. In fact, the ordinary person's worry, especially in this country, about the possibility of arbitrary action on the part of the Community tends to concentrate on the European Commission. The Commission on the other hand feels that it is harassed by the over-mighty civil servants of the big member states. It is they who so often fix the positions taken up by the ministerial representatives of governments in the meetings of the Council of Ministers. The upshot is that the Community's decisions in the Council of Ministers are often the outcome of a private triangular discussion between civil servants in Paris and in Bonn with members of the Commission staff in Brussels.

There is of course nothing very strange about all this; bureaucracies nowadays play a very large, though usually invisible, part in the legislative process. Parliaments are engaged in a constant struggle to assert their will against them. Too often their members are not equipped either with the necessary detailed knowledge or the supporting expert staff to make much of an impact on a powerful minister deploying the resources of a large government department. But the civil servants do not always win; and the mere risk of losing in a parliamentary battle is usually a significant factor in the process of government. It is this element of parliamentary pressure which needs to be brought into the affairs of the European Community. Various proposals have been made for strengthening the position of the European Parliament, including most recently those of the Vedel Committee.[4] In particular the Vedel scheme, which would compel the Council of Ministers to obtain the Parliament's consent before enacting European laws on certain subjects, would offer the parliamentarians a real opportunity to assert themselves. They would have to learn how to use it with skill, so that the Council of Ministers would be pushed into a continuous bargaining relationship with them on a widening range of subjects, in order to get the legislation which it, the Council, wanted, while accepting the need for compromise on other matters which the Parliament on its side regarded as essential.

But in the end, I am convinced that an effective European parliamentary system will depend on involving the national parliaments more and more in the process of European legislation. What is needed goes well beyond the proposals that are contemplated at Westminster for giving Parliament an effective means of checking on the laws that are in process of formulation by the European Community before decisions are made in Brussels. A determined Parliament will be able to do that quite readily – indeed it may find it has more effective influence on the preparation of this kind of legislation than on the shaping of many ordinary British laws.

The process that is required connects directly with the device of parallel uniform legislation enacted independently by the member states. What is necessary is to establish a network of parallel committees in the various parliaments concerned with

4. *The Enlargement of the Powers of the European Parliament* (Report Vedel), Brussels, 1972.

European matters, so that they act in unison with one another. The fact that the European Parliament is composed of national MPs with a double mandate puts it in an excellent position to orchestrate the whole process. Orchestration means in this context arranging joint meetings of parliamentary groups and committees drawn from different countries, working out a timetable which does not conflict with the main programmes of legislative business in the national parliaments, and, most important, arranging for parallel moves to be taken in the different national parliaments to put simultaneous pressure on several members of the Council of Ministers. This conception of parliamentary committee work is unfamiliar in this country; its closest analogy is with the United States Congress, whose Committees are certainly the most powerful parliamentary force in the contemporary democratic world. In the end European members of parliament, like other interest-groups in the Community, would develop their own powerful network of transnational relations.

Indeed I would be inclined to take this process to its logical conclusion and convert the European Parliament in Strasbourg into a kind of 'committee of committees' – or, more precisely, into a collection of European committees on the main topics of Community legislation, manned by MPs who are members of national parliamentary committees on the same subjects. I do not pretend that this would of itself solve the problem of more effective decision-making by the Community. But it would establish a common legislative process and a habit of joint action, building on the outstanding elements of strength in our existing democratic structures. It would also provide the visible evidence that effective opposition politics had been injected into the Community process. This process at present arouses the suspicions of the ordinary voter precisely because he feels that European decisions ought to be part of the rough and tumble of politics, and that instead they are being made behind his back. If his quite legitimate suspicions can be removed, these European decisions will more readily command his positive assent.

6

Wanted – an Instrument
for Crisis Management

In this chapter I shall explore some of the longer-term issues of the politics of the European Community.

First, Britain's entry is likely to cause a fundamental change in the power structure of the EEC. The fact that there will be three major powers in the Community, France, Britain and Germany, instead of just two will, in my view, make a profound difference to the way in which the whole operation is run in the future. This is because three is not just one more than two; a threesome is a quite different kind of forum for negotiation and bargaining. The ultimate threat of resignation by one of the members ceases to have the character of an absolute deterrent if it is clear that the Community could in the last resort survive with just two of the three. This is not an abstract point. I remember a comment made on an argument between the French and the Germans in an EEC committee on which the British were for the first time represented. A member of the staff of the European Commission said to me afterwards: 'The Germans felt liberated because they weren't constantly under the threat of being left face to face with the French.' It was a shrewd observation. How people feel in such encounters seeps through ultimately to the formulation of policies.

But my characterization of the new Community as a system dominated by three powers begs a lot of questions. For example, by what principle is Italy excluded from the big-power group, in spite of the fact that in terms of population, resources, and so on, it might be reckoned to belong in the same class as the other three? The answer that I would hazard is that it is largely because Italy perceives itself as a small power. Italian governments behave consistently in a recognizable style – a style which reflects a lack of confidence in their ability to take any serious international initiative, which in turn expresses a deeper doubt about their capacity to command the domestic support necessary to sustain a distinctive international posture. Various reasons can be advanced to explain these Italian political inhibitions; there are objective factors, social as well as economic, which contribute to the result.

But I must leave the analysis of causes; my concern is with the effect on the construction of Europe. I would only observe that it is not just a matter of the instability of governments. One notices that Holland, for example, which experiences cabinet crises that leave the country without a properly constituted government for six weeks at a time, is not on that account inhibited in the conduct of its foreign policy in a European context. The Dutch of course see themselves as a small power, but as a very active small power with a distinctive view on many international questions which they do not hesitate to press. One reason for the Dutch imperviousness to political crises is that everyone is confident that whether there is a functioning Prime Minister in The Hague or not, the institutions of the country – the civil service, the Parliament, the political parties and so on – are quite robust enough to ensure that on important issues effective decisions will be taken, and taken with proper regard to democratic principles. The Italian case is different. It is a fascinating question of political psychology how a country comes to assess itself as a greater or lesser power in international affairs. But the important point for the analysis of international relations is that this kind of self-assessment – always assuming that it is not grossly belied by subsequent performance – matters.

Inner Power Structure of the EEC

Ultimately, however, the difference between great powers and lesser ones in the Community context is, in my view, to be measured by the familiar old-fashioned criteria of international politics – by the size of the threat to the system which a nation can mount by withholding its cooperation, set against the loss of benefits which it derives from the system. Thus France in 1965–6, when it felt able to withdraw its representatives from Community bodies and caused considerable embarrassment to its partners, demonstrated that it was indeed a great power.

To take a hypothetical example at the other end of the scale, a threatened withdrawal by the Belgian Government would be annoying, even upsetting, but would not shake the Community to its foundations. At the same time, for Belgium it is recognized as a significant gain that it is able to participate through the Community in the making of important international decisions which would otherwise be made with little or no regard for Belgian interests. The weak bargaining position of the small countries makes for a readiness to accept the arrangements agreed among the big powers. They complain about not being consulted, but usually they don't reject the result. The officials of the big powers know this and act accordingly.

It seems likely that in the new European Community of the Nine the small powers may have rather more room for manoeuvre. This could well be one consequence of the increase in the big league powers of the Community from two to three. What is to be foreseen is both an improvement in performance and an increased instability in the actual working of the Community – better performance because there will be less simple blocking of Community decisions by one country as the bargaining becomes more fluid, accompanied by more overt conflict and friction. The upshot could be more strains on the structure but also more output from the machine. And in the more varied and flexible bargaining among the big three, France, Germany and Britain, the support or opposition of the small countries, especially if several of them gang up together, will more closely affect the balance of decision-making power than hitherto.

Another change that it is reasonable to anticipate is the adaptation of the role of the European Commission to the realities of the second phase of the construction of Europe. The point made in earlier chapters is that the ideological bias of the first phase, which purported to give the European Commission the status of an overlord in the process of European integration – an incipient European governmental power speaking with growing authority to obsolescent national governments – gets in the way of the efficient management of European affairs. The useful, indeed irreplaceable, functions of the Commission are firstly to provide the services of a skilful intermediary in all the varied forms of bargaining between the transnational interest-groups and organizations making up the Community, and secondly to be the innovator in the formulation of strategic policies for Europe. The danger is that because of the old pretensions to simple governmental power, the Commission may condemn itself to concentrate on the exercise of detailed regulatory functions – looking after agricultural regulations, seeing that the anti-trust rules are observed, that there is no cheating on European customs arrangements and on indirect taxes – instead of providing the long-term thinking and the tactical skills that are needed to keep pushing the process of European integration forward. The fascination of exercising direct governmental power may prove to be so great that the European Commission will confine itself to a role which finds its closest analogy in the federal regulatory agencies of the United States – the Federal Trade Commission, the Inter-State Commerce Commission, and so on. This would be because it preferred certain power here and now, however limited its extent, to the exercise of an uncertain but much more profound influence over the shape of political events in the future. In that case Europe will be the loser.

At this point it may be objected that the argument seeks to have it all ways: it looks to a Community which has more authority to make collective decisions on behalf of its members, which will be ready to cope with crises as they arrive, while at the same time it proposes to weaken the independent decision-making power of the European Commission. Yet it is also aimed to raise the political status of the European Commission, so that its members are persons of some acknowledged authority who can speak to the politicians of national governments on equal terms and make sure that they are listened to. Perhaps I can explain more closely how I see the Community functioning in the future by being more specific about the kind of European crisis that it may have to try to manage. The scenario that I shall use is of course imaginary, but it helps the exposition to make it as concrete as possible.

Consider a case in which democratic practice in one of the Community countries looks as if it might be about to break down; this goes back to the point made in the first chapter, that the European Community system can only function if there is broad agreement about social objectives and no major difference in social and political conditions among the member states. The kind of problem to which the Community will almost certainly have to respond some day can be conveniently illustrated by looking at a possible development in Italian politics. I choose Italy because it looks like the least stable democracy in Western Europe at present. Assume that the Christian Democrat Party, which has provided the base for all Italian governments since the war, is weakened or split. At the same time the Communist Party, which regularly polls a quarter of all the votes, further increases its electoral support. It wants, and is now given, an important place in a coalition government of the left. The immediate effect is to produce an extreme polarization of Italian politics, in the course of which armed groups of left-wing and right-wing supporters fight in the streets, the violence spreads, and in a number of cities government offices are occupied by guerrillas. The upshot is that a state of emergency is declared by a government in which the Communists are in a majority, and normal constitutional rights are suspended.

There is no need to paint in any more of the details of this gloomy scenario. The immediate question is whether Italy's partners in the Community are prepared to give the government there large-scale temporary credits to help it cope with the foreign-exchange crisis which, it is to be assumed, has accompanied the breakdown of social order. Beyond that there is the bigger issue: whether the Community collectively is ready to supply the kind of support – moral support by gestures and promises, as well as immediate practical measures – that will significantly increase the Italian Government's chances of functioning, or whether it takes the view that the only sensible course is to write off the Italians, at least temporarily, as members of the Community.

It would be an extremely hard decision. It would depend among other things on how far the stated democratic intentions of the Italian Communist Party were trusted, on the attitude taken by the Soviet bloc, on the possible effect of any Community action, or lack of it, on European military defence in the Mediterranean area. What is clear is that any decision taken by the countries of the European Community, including a decision to do nothing, would necessarily involve some of the most sensitive issues in the politics of these countries. If they are in fact able to act together in

a crisis of this kind it will only be because the habits of transnational collaboration and compromise between unofficial and
official agencies, starting with foreign offices and running through
the mass media, the trade unions, and the political clubs and
parties, are firmly established.

This would be a test of the supranational character of the European system – that is supranationality in the sense in which the
term is employed in this book, not depending on the establishment of a single supreme power standing above national governments, but on the organization of many bits and varieties of power
exercised by transnational groups which operate with a large
measure of autonomous initiative, even when their members are
themselves ultimately subject to the behests of governments. Thus
for example the development of such transnational links between
the officials working in the foreign offices of the nine member
countries is a precondition for effective crisis management in my
hypothetical scenario. For it is plainly not the kind of crisis which
the European Commission is, or should be, equipped to tackle. It
is a matter of intergovernmental politics at its most demanding.
Finally, it is to be observed that a political problem of this type in
one or other country of the Community – not necessarily in Italy
or involving the Communist Party – is something which is most
likely to present itself some time. And we cannot look to the early
establishment of a European political authority to solve it. We
shall have to rely on the habits of transnational collaboration,
backed by more frequent summit meetings of the heads of state,
for a long time yet. These are indeed the essential elements of the
Community method.

Uniform Laws versus Coordination of Policy

The Community does not move forward by capturing power from
the governments of national states and then transferring it to a
separate European institution, but by exercising compulsion on
the governments themselves to act together in new ways. Here
once again it was the experience of the first phase of the European
Common Market with its two main events, the establishment of a
customs union and of a common agricultural policy, both of

which transferred certain administrative powers from the national agencies to the central authority, which produced a distorted image of the future. The case is parallel to that of the European Parliament – originally seen as a kind of receptacle for powers to be forcibly surrendered by the individual national parliaments, but in practice likely to be most effective when it allies itself with national parliamentary power and helps to direct that power towards European purposes.

The institutions of the EEC as they exist today are an exceedingly strong instrument for imposing uniform rules on its member states – so strong indeed that there is some hesitation about using them on matters that are judged to be of national importance – but they are a meagre instrument for the coordination of national policies. The aim of uniformity was absolutely dominant in the first phase of the construction of Europe – uniform external tariffs, uniform agricultural prices, uniform margins of fluctuation for national currencies.

It seems probable that the model underlying the scheme of the founding fathers of the Community was excessively influenced by the experiences of federations with which they were familiar from European and American history. In Europe the successful federations, Germany and Switzerland, have been a device for bringing together people who already felt themselves in large measure to belong to a national group with a considerable degree of homogeneity. In America the ideal was the melting-pot – the creation of a new nation. The aim in these cases was to mould a new collective sense of identity *at the expense* of earlier loyalties – encouraging people to rub off some of their group individuality against one another, to identify themselves less as Bavarians because they were more German, to stop thinking about Virginia and concentrate on the United States. Now, in my view, the mood underlying the construction of Europe is different from this. The objective of those taking part in the enterprise is to integrate but not to merge – to maintain vigorously the individual character and separate identities of the national groups taking part.

Admittedly, some of these nations have been rather cavalier in their treatment of smaller regional units inside them, and one of the attractive aspects of the Community is that it provides a great deal more scope for the expression of local interests other than the purely national ones. But the nation will remain for many people – I suspect for the overwhelming majority of those involved – for a long time yet the primary centre of group loyalty. It is in this sense that the underlying principle of the European Community system, which is to secure equality of treatment between one's own national citizens and the much larger number of foreigners who are members of the European club, is to be seen as an essay in a more generous mode of civilized behaviour. National identity, while firmly maintained, is no longer accepted as a justifiable ground for discrimination in the treatment of persons. The principle has a long way to go yet, but in some ways the chief attraction of the European Community experiment is that it makes a start in setting new standards of treatment for people outside the range of one's immediate national loyalties.

All this suggests the need for rather less emphasis on detailed uniform regulation promulgated at the centre, and for rather more on devising arrangements for parallel action by national governments over broad areas of policy. The difference between the two methods can be seen very clearly in the current controversy over the approach to economic and monetary union. As was observed in Chapter 5, the Community has somehow allowed itself to get involved in a venture which attempts to fix its exchange rates in a rigid pattern, before it has begun seriously to engage in the much more important work of bringing the economic policies of the member states into harmony with one another. That will take a long time and will require a lot of difficult political decisions by the nine countries. Working on the exchange rates appears to be a short cut, but it isn't. It multiplies the differences and aggravates the frictions between the member states. It reflects the excessive reliance of the tacticians of the European Community on the blackmail principle of international politics: you manipulate your innocent partners into a position which is more compromising than they had imagined, in the hope that they will then find that they can't afford to opt out. If the stakes are big enough, as they plainly are in this case, they surely will. It is interesting to observe in the monetary debate how the French Government, in spite of its nationalist approach to the Community, finds itself, not for the first time, in a strange alliance with the European Commission, which is attracted by a technical device that promises to have the effect of subtracting from the individual nations some part of their independent power to manage their affairs. It will be apparent from the argument in the earlier chapters that I regard this preference for *technicity*, for automatic mechanisms which purport to bypass politics, as a profound error. Moreover, by treating these formal aspects of the approach to European monetary union as matters of supreme concern, the Community is diverted from the urgent task of working out a common position on the reform of the world monetary system, which is now in process of breaking down.

This leads to a more general observation about European policies at large. The Community's institutions and methods of conducting business were devised largely to deal with internal problems arising out of the relationships of the original six member countries with one another. The Community's external policies were largely neglected. It now turns out, in the 1970s, that the most urgent questions that the Community needs to tackle are concerned with its foreign policy. It has no practice in coping with these. It has hardly begun to try to define the relationship between itself and the different parts of the world outside. Indeed, until recently its foreign policy has had one over-riding aim – to be left alone to get on with the business of designing its own domestic arrangements.

That position was in any case becoming less and less acceptable to the rest of the world. And now the new Community of Nine, with its appendage of a European free-trade area, is going to be faced with an insistent demand for policy decisions covering its relations with the United States, with the Soviet bloc, with Latin America, with Asia and with Africa. But there is still a parochial tendency to look at these world problems primarily as an opportunity for adding to or improving some part of the Community's own internal structure. Typically, the instinctive reaction to the call for a new world monetary order to replace the Bretton Woods system was to see it as an opportunity to construct some extra piece of the edifice of European monetary union. In truth the urgency of the matter would require the Europeans to approach it by discovering first of all what minimum agreement was necessary among themselves in order to achieve a basis for negotiation with the United States. And this minimum is surely a great deal less than European monetary union.

In the same spirit the entry of Britain into the Community and the consequent need for a new set of relationships with the Commonwealth is treated as an occasion for enlarging and consolidating the established system of association agreements with former European colonies in Africa. What is now needed in reality is a fresh look at the relationship between the underdeveloped countries as a whole and the enlarged Community, taking account of the fact that this is by far the largest trading bloc in the world, that the nine member countries together provide much the biggest single market for the produce exported by the underdeveloped countries and supply them with more economic aid than the United States of America.

Indeed if one were searching for a subject on which the Community could most rapidly advance the practice of day-to-day collaboration in the management of national foreign policies, one could hardly do better than concentrate on the relationship of Western Europe with the underdeveloped countries. It would start with the great advantage that in all the countries concerned the stated objectives of development policy are broadly the same: all the member states are agreed on the primary aim of speeding up the rise in living standards in the countries of the Third World, and there is also agreement on at least some of the most promising means towards that end – notably the opportunity to sell more goods in the markets of the rich countries. Moreover, the underdeveloped countries do not raise the profound problems of international relations which are involved for example in Western Germany's approach to the Soviet bloc or in France's attitude towards the United States. I am not suggesting that the subject is friction-free, far from it; but it would not confront the West European countries with important differences of principle which might impede an attempt to arrive at joint policies on other subjects.

A European Opportunity in the Third World

Remembering that it is above all the practice of collaboration in its external affairs that the Community requires at this stage – learning by doing – the less-developed countries offer some advantages simply because of their sheer numbers. They account for over two thirds of all the nations with which the member states of the Community have diplomatic relations. And the greater part of the work that is done by their embassies and official representatives in these countries is connected in one way or another with economic development; this includes not only the finance of individual projects but also the provision of technical assistance and training and the grant of certain commercial preferences. There is of course besides a good deal of ordinary commercial business done in some of the less-developed countries, and European countries are interested in this too. However, as the Community becomes responsible for the management of a joint external commercial policy for all its nine members – a process which is to be set in motion in 1973 – the opportunities open to individual countries to obtain exclusive export advantages in these markets by offering them special commercial favours in return will be sharply restricted. The members of the Community will in any case have to take a fresh look at their arrangements for export promotion as their commercial relations with the rest of the world become a joint responsibility; they might well decide that it was convenient to hive off this activity from the ordinary work of their embassies and transfer it to a separate organization. This is a device which has already been found useful by some other countries, notably Japan.

Another aspect of external relations in which national sentiment tends to play a strong part is cultural activity. Here too some countries, Britain for example, have separated the organization whose job it is to conduct cultural relations, through art exhibitions, music, libraries and so on, from the diplomatic service.[1] It might be found convenient by other European embassies to hive

1. In our case the job is done by the British Council.

off this work too. In that case, with national culture and export promotion both out of the way, the rest of the work left to the representatives of the nine countries in the Third World would be a natural subject for joint action by the European Community.

My suggestion is that we should go beyond policy coordination in this particular sphere, to the more radical course of an executive merger – that we should amalgamate the actual instruments of policy abroad. If we did that, the appearance of substantial embassies of the European Community in more than half of the capitals of the world would itself be a visible demonstration of Western Europe's identity as a new factor in international relations. Of course there would be opposition to such a scheme as this from some quarters in the Community. But I suspect that outside France, and possibly Britain, these sentiments, which derive from a kind of afterglow of the period of empire, no longer have either much popular or elite appeal.

If the proposal were accepted the establishment of joint control over the external commercial relations of the Community countries, which is now imminent, would be complemented by a common European development policy. This would signify in effect the take-over by the European Community of the conduct of a large segment of the external relations of the member states. A suggestion of this kind would a few years back have been regarded as fantasy; if it has become practical politics today, the reason lies profoundly in the changed environment of international affairs. In Western Europe we now know that we have as nations lost the effective power to decide on war or peace – or to defend ourselves in the event of war against the most powerful of our possible enemies. In this situation many of the traditional functions of foreign policy have lost their earlier meaning. It is only because of a certain lag in our perceptions that we still automatically connect the activities of ministries of foreign affairs in Europe with the ultimate security of nations. In fact most of the business of foreign policy – other than the conduct of our relations with the super-powers and with a few other major states – no longer needs to have that exclusive national stamp that has marked it hitherto. The great bulk of it is neither very secret nor very sensitive. One sometimes feels that we are the victims of ceremonial diplomatic reflexes which we now find extraordinarily hard to change.

I do not ignore the fact that we have distinct and important national interests which figure in our relationships with certain countries. These have to be safeguarded by separate missions. We shall still need conventional British embassies in places like Moscow and Tokyo and perhaps a couple of dozen other capitals. But even there it will, I suspect, be seen to be convenient in the long run to establish a joint West European embassy to cope with our common commercial policies and with many other matters – finance and investment, science and technology, and ultimately such things as educational interchange and tourist travel – which the Community countries will increasingly manage in collaboration with one another.

The effect of all this on the behaviour of foreign offices in Britain and other West European countries would be considerable. Their staffs constitute a transnational group of great potential importance; once mobilized they would exercise a profound influence on the whole European enterprise. They would discover a need to involve themselves much more deeply in each other's ways of thinking, as part of the daily practice of collective action. They would become used to handling the small change of international politics in a common currency.

By way of conclusion it is worth recalling the underlying argument of this approach to Community politics. It starts by rejecting the short cut to European federation – 'the flight into the future' as the federalists call it. On the other hand it anticipates that there will be crises which will require collective decisions to be arrived at without long delays. The aim is to develop a capacity for coping with such crises as they arise. The earlier chapters have referred to a number of practical measures which, taken together, would make Western Europe significantly more capable of that. First, weighted majority voting should be gradually extended in the Council of Ministers to an increasing range of matters, and ultimately to all except a few highly sensitive national issues. Regular summit meetings between heads of governments would supplement this process. Second, a conscious effort should be made to exploit opportunities for making joint European decisions, outside as well as inside governments, which arise out of the massive growth of transnational relations. Knowing that you are irretrievably locked in with your neighbours wonderfully increases the propensity to act together. Third, the national bureaucracies should operate common foreign policies in joint embassies in the large number of countries in the Third World where promoting economic development is the paramount concern of member countries. Fourth, national M Ps should bring into being a more vigorous European parliamentary system based on transnational political parties, pressing the governments both in their national capitals and at the centre of the Community to think European.

I do not believe that we can establish in advance of the event the formal power and the institutions which will ensure that we manage Europe's future crises. What we can do is to create a mood and a set of habits which will make it feasible in a crisis situation to engage in joint European action on a scale that we have never approached before.

November 1972